T0305488

ARTIFICIAL INTELLIGENCE AND BLOCKCHAIN FOR SOCIAL IMPACT

Artificial Intelligence and Blockchain for Social Impact provides an accessible overview of artificial intelligence (AI) and blockchain technologies and explores their applications for social enterprise and impact investing.

The opening chapter introduces the impact space, exploring different social business models, the role of technology, the impact investing market and general problems in the space. The remainder of this book falls into two paths: the first focusing on AI and the other looking at the blockchain technology. Providing introductions to each of these technologies and their histories, the author goes on to examine them from the perspectives of social business models and impact finance. A concluding chapter explores AI and cryptocurrencies in the impact space in the future. Readers are supported with international case studies and other student-friendly features.

Situated at the intersection between technology, fintech, social enterprise, impact investing and social impact, this book is a valuable resource for upper-level courses across all these areas. It also offers an introduction to this emerging topic for researchers and business professionals.

Online teaching resources to accompany this book include instructor lecture slides and datasets.

Wolfgang Spiess-Knafl is Co-Director of the European Center for Social Finance at the Munich Business School and Managing Director of Next Generation Impact in Vienna. Since completing his doctorate on 'financing social enterprises' at the Technical University of Munich, he has worked on the development of the social finance market for the European Commission and written studies on social finance for the European Parliament or the European Liberal Forum, among others. In 2017, he co-authored a book on impact investing. He regularly advises social finance intermediaries and is currently developing artificial intelligence (AI) and blockchain-based concepts for the impact sector.

ARTIFICIAL INTELLIGENCE AND BLOCKCHAIN FOR SOCIAL IMPACT

Social Business Models and Impact Finance

Wolfgang Spiess-Knafl

Routledge
Taylor & Francis Group

LONDON AND NEW YORK

Cover image: Aerial view of crowd connected by lines, Orbon Alija

First published 2023
by Routledge
4 Park Square, Milton Park, Abingdon, Oxon OX14 4RN

and by Routledge
605 Third Avenue, New York, NY 10158

Routledge is an imprint of the Taylor & Francis Group, an informa business

© 2023 Wolfgang Spiess-Knafl

British Library Cataloguing-in-Publication Data
A catalogue record for this book is available from the British Library

Library of Congress Cataloging-in-Publication Data
Names: Spiess-Knafl, Wolfgang, author.
Title: Artificial intelligence and blockchain for social impact : social business
models and impact finance / Wolfgang Spiess-Knafl.
Description: New York, NY : Routledge, 2023. |
Includes bibliographical references and index. |
Identifiers: LCCN 2022023984 | ISBN 9781032112206 (hardback) |
ISBN 9781032112190 (paperback) | ISBN 9781003218913 (ebook)
Subjects: LCSH: Social entrepreneurship. | Finance–Moral and ethical aspects. |
Artificial intelligence–Social aspects. | Blockchains (Databases)–Social aspects.
Classification: LCC HD60 .S673 2023 | DDC 338/.04–dc23/eng/20220523
LC record available at https://lccn.loc.gov/2022023984

ISBN: 978-1-032-11220-6 (hbk)
ISBN: 978-1-032-11219-0 (pbk)
ISBN: 978-1-003-21891-3 (ebk)

DOI: 10.4324/9781003218913

Typeset in Bembo
by Newgen Publishing UK

Access the Support Material: www.routledge.com/9781032112190

CONTENTS

FIGURES

TABLES

1

INTRODUCING THE IMPACT SPACE

1.1 Introduction

The emergence of the blockchain technology and artificial intelligence (AI) is among the most promising and fascinating developments of our time. Both technologies can be deployed and implemented to generate social value and impact as they enable a new generation of business models and financing instruments. Some even mention it as the playground of the century. It is a fast-evolving space, and social science could even enter a golden age with the amount of data available to policymakers, citizen, and organizations (Domingos 2015).

Technologies per se are not impactful, and it always remains to be seen how they are implemented. It is obvious that technologies can have negative and positive effects on many aspects of daily life.

Some are now talking about multiple crises which are happening at the same time. We are facing a democracy crisis, a climate crisis, an inequality crisis, and a public health crisis related to the Covid-19 pandemic and armed conflicts in the Middle East and Eastern Europe, among others.

Consider the democracy crisis. Globally, a decline in trust toward politicians and the political processes can be observed. It has to do with corruption, a lack of transparency, a loss of independent media, and pressure on independent reporting. There is no easy way to fix this problem, but AI can help to identify fake or misleading news. At the same, AI is used to create fake images, videos, and voice recordings. Blockchain technologies can help to monitor cash payments in the international aid area or support voting systems.

Inequality is often cited as a major social challenge. The developments and numbers have been well documented (Piketty 2018). For example, it has been shown that digital tools help to exacerbate global inequalities (Bauer 2018). This is especially the case for AI as employees and entrepreneurs with digital skills will

DOI: 10.4324/9781003218913-1

stand to profit disproportionately from new digital skills as employers and clients will pay wage premiums for their services.

Blockchain technologies can also have an impact on global inequality. It is rumored that it contributed to rising electricity prices in regions where individuals and companies run mining operations for blockchain networks.

1.2 Global differences in terms of impact

Nonprofit organizations or socially oriented organizations in general have been active for many centuries. Early examples are Friedrich Wilhelm Raiffeisen who is often cited as the inventor of the microfinance system and an inspiration for Muhammad Yunus.

Social entrepreneurs also include Frances Nightingale or Maria Montessori which worked toward improving healthcare for the sick and education for the children. The quakers were also often cited as early examples as activists (Busch et al. 2021).

The history knows many examples of paternalistic entrepreneurs who offered additional benefits to their employees. Siemens, Krupp, Lever, and Cadbury were known for running housing schemes or organizing travels for employees more than 100 years ago. This led the historian Trentmann (2016) to conclude that humanitarianism was good business. It led to fewer stoppages, higher retention, and higher productivity. It makes sense to conclude that these gains outweigh related costs. Trentmann (2016) also added that exploitation was a dominant strategy when owners depended mainly on unskilled labor. This is an interesting historical finding, and it is interesting to note that similar patterns can also be found today adding to the complexity of the field.

Since the 1980s, there have been numerous parallel trends. For example, the Apartheid system led to the creation of cooperatives which wanted to take actions against it. The 1980s also saw the commercialization of the nonprofit sector. This was partly driven by public authorities which started to put pressure on the nonprofit sector by using budgeting techniques as well as tendering procedures for the procurement of social services. As nonprofit organizations had to cover budget cuts, they implemented entrepreneurial income-generating activities (Weisbrod 1998).

The impact space is quite unique in every country and changes over time. The literature usually covers the American and the European perspectives when it comes to impact. The early 2000s saw an increased interest in social enterprises. The first philanthropists were experimenting and pioneering new approaches. The main idea was to support a few selected social enterprises instead of a large number of organizations and led to the development of the venture philanthropy field (Letts, Ryan, and Grossman 1997).

The Nobel Prize for Muhammad Yunus and the Grameen Bank he founded also supported the development and led to increased media interest in this topic. Public authorities started to support these initiatives. Some examples include Barack Obama's Office for Social Innovation, the European Commission's "Social Business

Initiative" (SBI) or the Social Impact Investment Taskforce announced by David Cameron at the G8 Social Impact Investment Forum in 2013.

In parallel, there were trends to build and integrate social values in traditional companies. Shared value is one such approach (Porter and Kramer 2019).

Each geographical area has its own traditions and legacies. The most diverse approaches can be observed in Europe. While countries such as France or Belgium have a long history of an "économie sociale" with strong involvement of cooperatives and civil society, the post-communist countries in Eastern Europe are still working on developing ecosystems and modern social economies (Borzaga et al. 2020). There are many different approaches to explain these differences. For example, philanthropy and giving is usually developed over generations, and there have been less opportunities to create generational wealth across many of the Eastern European countries.

In Russia, companies, foundations, and the nonprofit sector face specific expectations from the national and local governments as well as from the general public. Some of the expectations for companies even date back to Soviet times and include the provision of local social and other public services (e.g., Jakobson, Toepler, and Mersianova 2018; Skokova, Pape, and Krasnopolskaya 2018).

China is a country which has received much attention related to developments in philanthropy and civil society in recent years. Hu and Sidel (2020) analyze the role of the civil society in responding to the Covid-19 pandemic and find that most volunteering were managed by state agencies or party branches. All volunteers were required to submit to the arrangement of party committees and government departments. It is thus clear that the environment for civil society organizations is more restrictive than in other countries.

Arab-speaking countries have a long history of charity and society rooted in Islamic traditions, and Islamic finance is a separate and quickly emerging research field (e.g., Hassan and Mollah 2018; Biancone and Radwan 2019).

Social enterprises also play a prominent role in emerging markets. There has been a wave of "Bottom of the Pyramid" business cases popularized as a concept by Prahalad, Prahalad, and Fruehauf in 2005. However, it has been observed since then that most concepts ignore the bottom of the pyramid but rather focus on the middle layers of the pyramid. The recent case of Abraaj is a good reminder that business acumens and strategies are not able to solve any given social problem (Clark and Louch 2021).

1.3 Development of social problems over time

Social problems also evolve over time. At the beginning, experts, pressure groups, or activist campaigns raise awareness for a certain topic. If these awareness-raising campaigns and activities are successful, the media coverage will help to spread awareness and help to build public recognition of the problem. In a next step, it can either be put on the political agenda or tackled by foundations, companies, or the civil society. This "career" of social problems can be observed for most social problems (Schetsche 2014). The deforestation of the Amazonas, the tragedy of HIV/AIDS, or the danger of climate change have all been first voiced by groups of individuals.

Governments and international organizations have been supportive of the development of social business models and social enterprises. They fund social impact bonds, incubator programs for social start-ups, and rolled out guarantee programs for the social finance market. Public authorities see the potential to improve society well-being and find it attractive to leverage private capital for the development of the sector.

The United Nations developed one of the key frameworks. The Sustainable Development Goals (SDGs) were introduced in 2015. The SDGs include 17 goals and 169 targets that address a range of different areas such as poverty, education, inequality, or environmental degradation.[1] Most of the areas are closely connected.

Education is a good example, and its effects have been widely studied (e.g., Barker et al. 2005; Cutler and Lleras-Muney 2006; Banerjee et al. 2007; Montenegro and Patrinos 2013). Better educational outcomes improve lifetime earnings of the children later in life and consequently lead to lower poverty rates. Persons with higher incomes can also spend more on food of higher nutritional quality. Better nutrition also leads to more income-generation opportunities for the adults and also improves the learning results of the children in the household.

More income and less hunger are also associated with better health and well-being. However, there is also a relationship between education and health as more knowledge leads to better health.

The network of targets can also be expanded across all targets. For example, better education helps girls to better understand family planning which impacts gender equality.

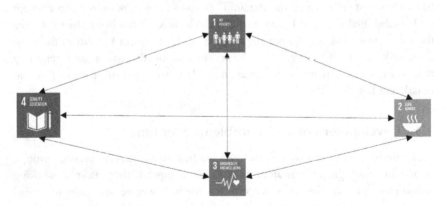

FIGURE 1.1 Network of targets for the SDGs

Source: Own illustration

An important aspect is that policy objectives should be measured. Social progress has been measured for a long time, and there are very good estimates for indicators such as life expectancies, income levels, or even happiness.

Some of the 169 targets of the 2030 Agenda for Sustainable Development are already measured globally. The SDG target 3.1 postulates that by 2030, the global maternal mortality ratio should be reduced to less than 70 per 100,000 live births. This is a target with numbers which are easily available. Statistical authorities routinely track this number, and it is thus widely available.

The SDG target 4.6 states that by 2030, all youth and a substantial proportion of adults, both men and women, should achieve literacy and numeracy. It measures the progress by tracking the percentage of population achieving a certain level of literacy and numeracy skills. This is already tracked by national statistical authorities.

However, there are other targets which are not easily available and more difficult to measure. For example, the SDG target 9.1.1 is focused on increasing the number of people living within 2 kilometers of an all-season road. Obviously, this is mainly relevant for the rural areas across Latin America, Africa, and Asia.

The current approaches rely on household surveys and consultations with various stakeholders. The data are available but highly fragmented. Ilie, Brovelli, and Coetzee (2019) propose a model which is built on open-source software and open-geospatial data. However, it still includes substantial manual work and might be cost-prohibitive.

AI can contribute to an automatic mapping and measurement of this target. AI-based tools use satellite data to identify settlements and calculate the number of inhabitants. The same satellite data can also be used to identify all-season roads and calculate how far away settlements are from these roads.

1.4 The role of technology in the fight against climate change

Climate change will continue to impact our lives slowly and consistently. Changing weather patterns will impact agricultural yields, the frequency of natural disasters, or the emergence of urban heat islands, among others.

It is obvious that technology alone will not help to reduce carbon emissions, but there are many opportunities to use these technologies in the fight against climate change. Ride-sharing and carpooling need AI-based tools to help combine single rides. Smart thermostats need to learn about the weather patterns, the dynamics of the heating system, and the usual presence of the residents to ensure that the house is warm enough once they are coming home from the office, the factory, or school. Efficient urban farming needs a smart control system for water and fertilizer, among others.

The most promising concepts involving renewable energies are built on energy communities operated by private individuals in neighborhoods (Yahaya et al. 2020). One of the problems involves the payment structures as deliveries sometimes amount to only a few cents. Blockchain technologies can help to structure the micropayments or at least document the flows of electricity.

A recent development is programs which aim to support the transformation of the economy to a lower level of carbon emissions. There are many programs which support the transformation, and a majority of citizens usually indicate that they are taking personal action to fight climate change. The current pandemic might obscure some of the problems, but climate change will remain one of the biggest themes for the foreseeable future.

Climate change impacts our lives slowly but consistently. Through changing weather patterns, it not only impacts agricultural yields and the frequency of natural disasters but also the development of urban heat islands among other things.

The topic has received much more attention over the last three decades. An emerging sense of the future costs of today's emissions has also slowly developed and contributed to the creation of a sense of urgency. One estimate puts the social costs of one ton of emissions at $42 (Auffhammer 2018).[2]

Obviously, the costs vary heavily depending on the discount rates and the underlying model. A bit simplified, these models start with CO_2 emissions and model the carbon cycle with redistributions around the atmosphere and the oceans. This results in changes in sea levels, ocean currents, or general warming and consequently impacts ecosystems, agriculture, or tourisms and costs to society (Nordhaus and Sztorc 2013).

The cascading effects of climate change have been widely popularized by Wallace-Wells (2019). Lawrence et al. (2020) discuss these effects in their example for New Zealand and describe it in this example of the heavy rainfall cascade. The effects described might be very specific but exemplify the chain of events:

> More frequent higher-intensity rainfall, compounded by infill housing, increases exposure by overwhelming stormwater systems. This leads to localised flooding; inflow of stormwater to wastewater systems; damage to property, roads, and stormwater networks; public health risks; sedimentation; and potential death and injury. Older low-lying settlements with aging gravity stormwater systems and houses built close to waterways or with floors close to the ground are particularly susceptible. Community intolerance accelerates in response to repeat flooding, disruption, cost of evacuations, and the ineffectiveness of agencies' responses. Current funding models to navigate local government debt limits and the ability of communities to absorb rates increases become stressed, and homeowners who want to move, face difficulty selling their property and feel stuck. The time lag required to establish new funding arrangements for addressing the ongoing impacts creates general community stress and frustration.

Climate change is mainly driven by the emission of greenhouse gases (GHGs).[3] Consequently, one of the main strategies to mitigate climate change is to reduce GHG emissions. At the same time, the same strategies also help to reduce pollution and waste.

There are thousands of potential ways to reduce GHG emissions. It can include the insulation of buildings, less consumption of meat, less waste in the food supply chain, better use of old materials or increased use of bicycles to mention just a few.

AI and blockchain technologies can contribute to reducing the effects of climate change. The following table shows solutions to reduce carbon emissions and the potential reductions in emissions.

Impact can be created across different domains and can include ecological as well as social objectives. It is an interesting question how both objectives overlap. There are three aspects to consider in this relationship.

The first aspect is that some concepts need a social business model to work. The involvement of volunteers or access to non-market resources might not be possible with a for-profit business model. In some cases, concepts are only able to work when they gain the trust of the stakeholders or include marginalized target groups. Social enterprises are known for their capabilities in this field. Examples can be found of alternative forms of mobility, carbon footprint trackers, regional food production, urban farming, or the circular economy.

TABLE 1.1 Selected solutions to reduce GHG emissions

Solution	Description	Plausible-Optimum Scenario Emissions Reduction (GtCO2-eq)
Reduced food waste	Minimizing food loss and wastage throughout the food supply chain from harvest to consumption	70.5–93.7
Plant-rich diets	Eating more plant-based foods and fewer animal proteins and products (e.g., meat, dairy)	66.1–87.0
Ride-sharing	Using ride-sharing services and/or carpooling	6.9–29.5
Bicycle infrastructure	Biking to destinations in cities instead of using cars	2.3–11.4
Walkable cities	Walking to destinations in cities instead of using cars	2.9–11.1
Household water saving	Using water saving devices in homes such as low-flow showerheads	4.6–6.3
Smart thermostats	Using devices that reduce heating and cooling demand through sensors and settings in the home	2.6–5.8
Household recycling and recycled paper	Recycling paper, metal, plastic, and glass materials	3.7–5.5

Source: Williamson et al. (2018).

The distribution of ugly fruits is a good example. Consider the problem of "ugly fruits" which are hard to sell in supermarkets. Ribeiro et al. (2018) discuss the example of Fruta Feia in Portugal.[4] It is basically a concept that markets and distributes aesthetically 'non-standard' ugly fruits ("fruta feia" in Portuguese) to consumers. There are other similar social enterprises and marketing campaigns in other countries.

It is a cooperative where consumers pay an annual fee of €5 and ~€4 for a box that contains 3–4 kg of different fruits. Volunteers help in the distribution process and are rewarded with a weekly box for their efforts. As of early 2022, they have more than 7,700 customers.

The second aspect group involves those concepts that combine social and environmental targets. This is sometimes referred to as the "triple bottom line" (Norman and MacDonald 2004) or as a "green collar army" (Vickers and Lyon 2014). Concepts include the circular economy or concepts related to waste recovery or upcycling which both offer many entry-level job opportunities.

The third group involves those concepts that try to mitigate the impact of climate change on society. Societies need to adapt to changing realities, but there is also a need to ensure that any transition to a low-carbon economy is fair and inclusive. Urban heat islands impact society through higher mortality rates, the heat-induced reduction of physical activities with its accompanying health issues, and some even argue an increased level of conflict. It also impacts insurance rates, income opportunities, migration patterns, or life quality through high pollution levels (e.g., Lawrence et al. 2020).

One key issue is that climate change is a slow-moving process. It might take years or decades to realize that agriculture is not feasible anymore or that areas do not offer enough income opportunities or insurance rates are restrictively high.

1.5 Definition of impact

Social impact is harder to define than environmental impact. It is relatively easy to measure one ton of GHG emissions as it is standardized and the same in Dhaka or in Stockholm. This also helped to scale the market for GHG emissions with mandatory and voluntary markets.

However, social inclusion, quality education, sustainable employment, or equitable healthcare are all not standardized and differently assessed in Rio de Janeiro than in Seattle. There are many contextual, moral, and normative differences to consider.

This leaves us with the question what impact is. In a most basic definition, impact is what improves the life of people.

The other part is related to 'social' which means that enterprises

have explicit social aims such as job creation, training or the provision of local services. They have strong social values and mission, including a commitment to local capacity building. They are accountable to their members and the wider community for their social, environmental and economic impact.

Shaw and Carter 2007

Becker and Shadbegian (2008) define the environmental or green sector as "the manufacture of products, performance of services and the construction of projects used, or that potentially could be used, for measuring, preventing, limiting, or correcting environmental damage to air, water, and soil" as well as "services related to the removal, transportation, storage, or abatement of waste, noise, and other contaminants." As already mentioned, the environmental sector has some advantages over the social sector as the impact is quite uniformly comparable globally. Emissions are standardized, whereas educational standards or living standards depend on the regional context.

There are different impact pathways and theories of change which define how a certain intervention or project might lead to a better situation for the target group. Take the example of attendance rates of children in rural Kenya which are positively related to educational outcomes. There are many interventions to increase this number (Snilstveit et al. 2017).

Interventions focusing on the children and the household might provide scholarships or cash transfers, provide information about the benefits of education, or run school-feeding programs. School-feeding programs improve children's health which lead to fewer absences or improved concentration and ability to learn. Scholarships lower the costs of schooling for the parents and increase access to schooling.

On a system level, organizations and public authorities can hire additional teachers, provide materials for schools, or introduce school-based management systems. Better-run schools and better teachers lead to an improved learning environment which should positively impact the educational outcomes of the schoolchildren.

Such an understanding also allows to measure the impact of capital. Randomized control trials (RCTs) have been used to assess how impactful certain interventions are (Kremer, Brannen, and Glennerster 2013). For example, RCTs find that a free school uniform reduces dropout rates among girls by 3.1%. $100 dollars spent on school-based deworming was found to generate 14 additional years of schooling.

In general, the term 'impact' is used rather freely. Usually, people follow an approach called the I-O-O-I logic with the following elements (e.g., Rosenzweig 2004; Jackson and Harji 2016)

- Input
- Activity
- Output
- Outcome
- Impact

Input is those resources that are used to achieve the objectives. It can include investments or other non-monetary resources. Activity is those actions or tasks which are undertaken to achieve the objectives of the project or organization.

The differentiation between output, outcome, and impact is important to assess the success of the project or organization. The output is those products and services which are a result of the activities undertaken. It can include the number of loans provided, the number of lessons, or the number of publications. Output is those results which can be most easily measured.

Outcomes are the changes to the social system and include aspects such as the household income after the provision of the loan or the educational outcomes such as better test results or higher attendance rates.

However, sometimes these changes occur anyway. For example, household incomes are usually increasing in line with gross domestic product (GDP) growth, and it is necessary to assess the changes that follow from the activities undertaken.

It is complicated to assess every detail of the impact, and some changes take a long time to take effect. For example, it might take decades to assess the impact on crime reduction for preschool activities. There are also different levels of evidence for the models. On the most basic level, there is anecdotal evidence followed by structured interviews. RCTs often called the gold standard as they analyze certain interventions and compare two groups with a randomized approach.

1.6 Social business models

Social business models are often tied to the creation of social impact. In the literature, social business, social enterprises, and social ventures are commonly used synonymously. Social entrepreneurship is the use of entrepreneurial and business methods to achieve and create social value. There are many different definitions for social entrepreneurship, social enterprises, and social entrepreneurs.

Social entrepreneurship is the process of identifying opportunities and organizations to exploit these opportunities. These organizations are social enterprises which are created by social entrepreneurs.

Dees (1998) defines social entrepreneurs as change agents who adopt a mission to create social value, recognize opportunities to serve that mission, and act boldly without being limited by currently available resources. This definition is rather idealistic as it states that social entrepreneurs act relentlessly, transparently, and are continuously innovating. It also focuses on the person of the entrepreneur.

Zahra et al. (2009) define social entrepreneurship as "the activities and processes undertaken to discover, define, and exploit opportunities in order to enhance social wealth by creating new ventures or managing existing organizations in an innovative manner." It focuses on the activities from discovering opportunities to building organizations.

Martin and Osberg (2007) introduce an interesting aspect as they see social entrepreneurship in more systemic ways. It is the identification of stable but unjust equilibria and the search to identify and forge new stable equilibria which improve the lives of those previously marginalized.

A common definition is used by the European institutions such as the European Commission or the European Investment Fund (European Union 2013). It is a rather inclusive definition which includes cooperatives, nonprofits, and traditional companies. It is therefore independent of the legal form and puts the emphasis on the output or the mode of production. In addition, there is a restriction on how profits have to be used and the social objective has to be the primary objective. There are also requirements on accountability and transparency.

It is an interesting definition as it ignores the legal form. Any legal form can be defined as a social enterprise. Some other jurisdictions have similar clauses which include, for example, asset locks. Definition should also be flexible as social enterprises respond to changing social circumstances as well (Mittermaier, Shepherd, and Patzelt 2021).

TABLE 1.2 Work distribution in society

Actors	Distinct Role in Economic System	Dominant Institutional Goal	Dominant Logic of Action
Governments	Centralized mechanism through which the infrastructure of the economic system is created and enforced	Defend public interest	Regulation
Business	Distributed mechanism through which society's resources and skills are allocated to the most valued activities	Create sustainable advantage	Control
Charity	Distributed mechanism through which economic outcomes are made more equitable despite uneven resource endowments	Support disadvantaged populations	Goodwill
Commercial entrepreneurship	Distributed mechanism through which neglected opportunities for profits are explored	Appropriate value for stakeholders	Innovation
Social activism	Distributed mechanism through which behaviors that bring negative externalities are selected out	Change social system	Political action
Social entrepreneurship	Distributed mechanism through which neglected positive externalities are internalized in the economic system	Deliver sustainable solution	Empowerment

Source: Santos (2012).

Santos (2012) proposed a positive theory which defines a distinct role and dominant logics for each actor in society.

1.7 Social innovation and the role of technology

Social innovation is understood quite broadly. Some see the introduction of gay marriage as social innovation, while others refer to new forms of urban mobility as social innovation. There are thus various approaches to define social innovation (e.g., Rüede and Lurtz 2012; João-Roland and Granados 2020).

A commonly used definition was developed by Phills, Deiglmeier, and Miller (2008) which sees social innovation as a "novel solution to a social problem that is more effective, efficient, sustainable, or just than existing solutions and for which the value created accrues primarily to society as a whole rather than private individuals." It highlights the novelty of a solution which is related to a social problem. It also includes a requirement that not all profits should accrue to the owners of the organizations but to the general public. This is consistent with other definitions in this sector and implies especially that non-defined persons also benefit from the products and services.

Jansen, Mast, and Spiess-Knafl (2021) analyze the investment portfolios of social venture capital funds. They find that out of 397 investments, 203 focused on technology. This is surprising as venture capital funds have an almost complete focus on technology. This means that there is still a need for smart non-tech-focused investments in this space. These investments include social housing, biogas facilities, or agriculture investment in dairy brands or irrigation systems.

It was also obvious that the employed technology was rather lower tech than the technology usually employed by those in the venture capital industry. It might be explained by the decreasing costs of technology. Costs decrease over time and make it easier to be implemented in other industries.

Coppi (2021) argues in a similar way saying that the skill set required to build distributed ledgers remains too expensive for the nonprofit and public sectors. In addition, it is mostly an additional product and only rarely the core of the vision and organization itself.

There is a large body of literature focusing on digitalization. We have seen digitalization tendencies for the last 30 years, and some are even arguing that we are entering the second half of the digitalization.

In addition, it is hard to imagine a technology which has no economic, societal, or political impact (Manski and Bauwens 2020). The same applies for AI and the blockchain technology.

New technologies are often accompanied by media campaigns which highlight the positive and societal aspects. For example, organizations and companies promoting the drone technology often highlighted the positive impact for rural areas with use cases such as medicine delivery for islands or remote areas in emerging countries.

Over the last years, we have seen more digital social business models. This is driven by the fact that digital tools are becoming more widespread and easier to use. Digital technologies are used to innovate a business model, add new revenue streams, and exploit new opportunities (Parida, Sjödin, and Reim 2019).

Organizations and companies developing digital social business models have more flexibility in structuring them. For example, they can implement more inclusive governance models or develop narratives which are more attractive for the users (Jansen, Mast, and Spiess-Knafl 2021).

Overall, there are many topics which need to be addressed in the sector such as the low quality of existing data, a lack of skills to implement new technologies, and data security. It is still hard to scale solutions to solve certain problems. Usually, solutions work in a certain context and environment as they depend on personal relationships and access to networks.

Across the social sector, only a few organizations are using advanced data analytics tools. In the wider social field, we are finding issues with resistance. In one case, a labor market agency introduced an algorithm to allocate resources to the unemployed. In principle, it makes sense, but it was met with strong resistance based on questions around the objectivity and neutrality of the model (Allhutter et al. 2020).

Moreover, there are issues with the data quality. In many cases, information is entered manually and on paper. It is not easy to transfer them digitally and ensure a high quality of the data. A typical organization providing training for young unemployed persons illustrates the point. The participants fill out questionnaires on paper, and there are issues with the manual entry of these data in digital sheets. Moreover, it is often not possible to track the progress of individuals over time as there are privacy issues or no possibilities to track them.

1.8 Emerging opportunities based on AI and blockchain technology

AI enables a new generation of business models. One of the first use cases of neural networks was the field of speech recognition. It is easy to understand why this was the case. It is almost impossible to come up with rules to separate certain sounds and transcribe them into text in every language. AI systems have been found to be very accurate in this field.

AI can also be used in the financing field. Finance is a natural environment for AI-based applications as there is plenty of data but usually only one result which is of interest. All finance-related applications somehow try to either reduce the risk or increase the potential financial returns for their investors.

Environmental, social, and governance (ESG) data providers use AI-based tools to analyze thousands of data sources and millions of pages and news articles to find clues and information which has not been identified manually. They try to assess the risk related to environment-, social-, or governance-related issues as companies might not be transparent about their pollution levels or human rights records. These unidentified risks can be costly for investors if it becomes public.

Individuals and companies applying for loans usually need to show a credit history to be eligible for loans by a bank or another financial institution. This also applies for credit cards or installment payment by retail companies. Some AI-based concepts use alternative data to build credit scores for individuals and companies. For example, it might be perfectly fine to assess the payment patterns for utilities as an alternative data point to prove the creditworthiness of individuals.

The blockchain technology is a social technology as it is based on human perception and the acceptance of certain mechanisms.[5] There is little value for cryptocurrencies if they are not widely accepted. It is still surprising how Bitcoin gained traction since its launch in 2009. It is a typical example of how a new technology is spread over time. It involves a lot of outreach activities, conferences, and networking.

At the core, the blockchain technology is a simple tool to secure data and structure decisions. A completely anonymous crowd can work together and transact without any central authority. This also attracted a certain type of individuals to this field.

Over time, the narrative of the field changed. Low transaction costs were a major theme in the early 2010s. The major themes in the early 2020s are non-fungible tokens (NFTs), decentralized finance (DeFi), and cryptocurrencies as an institutional asset class.

The blockchain technology offers a very rich design space. Some are referring to this design space as Web3 as a new architectural model reflecting the degree of centralization. Web1 had a decentralized nature, while the major platforms centralized many of the services and infrastructure in the Web2. Web3 is the promise to give control and potentially ownership back to the users.

The blockchain technology is best known for its cryptocurrencies such as Bitcoin and Ether and its implementation in the Decentralized Finance (DeFi) space. It enables new and decentralized forms of financing and the total value of the DeFi space reached more than $100 billion in 2021. The blockchain technology enables new business models for financial institutions and companies to use new fundraising tools. The blockchain technology also enables new business models such as decentralized judicial systems, decentralized autonomous organizations, supply chain transparency, or impact tracking, among others.

1.9 The impact investing market

Over the last 20 years, a capital market for the financing of social impact emerged. It started with foundations which considered how to better fund innovative social enterprises. The term "impact investing" was coined in 2007 at a meeting organized by the Rockefeller Foundation (Höchstädter and Scheck 2015).

A common definition from the Global Impact Investment Network defines impact investing as (GIIN 2009):

> Investments made with the intention to generate positive, measurable social and environmental impact alongside a financial return.

It includes two main aspects. There should be a positive financial return and a measurable social and environmental impact. The definition shown above is an indication that there is a spectrum of investment opportunities. For example, philanthropy is mainly concerned with impact goals, and there is always a full loss of capital.

Impact finance is defined as finance related to the generation and creation of social and environmental impact. It includes all financing instruments and mechanisms suitable to achieve these objectives.

Actors in the traditional financial markets usually maximize their financial returns and do not consider impact goals. For example, the financing of a new coal mine is not problematic as the financial returns might be positive. However, there might be large risks related to the assets which might result in substantial losses in the coming years. Therefore, investors increasingly try to integrate environmental and social risks in their investment decisions.

It is well understood that there is a relationship between finance and entrepreneurship and that a lack of finance is a growth barrier for start-ups (e.g., Block et al. 2018). The same applies for the impact investing market as well (Spiess-Knafl and Scheck 2019). On the supply side of the impact investment market, there are capital owners who are interested in funding social projects. Each of these capital providers has different return expectations.

One of the more important groups is foundations who want to invest part of their assets. Foundations are also giving grants to enterprises to support their activities and capacity building. There are also professional and institutional investors such as banks, pension funds, or insurance companies who manage capital on behalf of their clients. They aim to generate profits and react to demands from their clients. The last group is retail and crowd investors. They want to support local or social initiatives and are also attracted by financial returns.

Capital owners have different motivations to invest in the impact space. Some argue that a diversity of assets is helpful to reduce the risks. For example, microfinance returns show little statistical relationship with other global markets and can be used to construct more efficient portfolios (Krauss and Walter 2009; Galema, Lensink, and Spierdijk 2011).

For foundations and family office, impact finance might increase the alignment of its investment activities. It can often be observed that investors have large equity stakes in industries which contribute heavily to climate change and use dividends to support climate projects. Obviously, this lack of alignment can create tensions between the different activities, and this led some to explore options to align the capital stock of the foundation with its mission.

It is not an easy undertaking as there are many factors preventing foundations to align their activities. Among these factors are considerations around fiduciary duties, lack of internal skills, and missing market infrastructures (Zolfaghari and Hand 2021).

Another group is those who make a conscious decision to give up some percentages of their financial returns for the social impact. In general, the studies and results are rather mixed. It depends on the sample, the methodology, and the timing. McLachlan and Gardner (2004) find differences between conventional and socially responsible investors. The sample was rather small, but it showed that socially responsible investors rate ethical issues higher than conventional investors. Other areas such as age categories showed no significant differences.

Cheah et al. (2011) find that younger and female investors are more likely to consider social objectives in their investment decisions. Interestingly, they also find that younger investors with high income and higher education levels see socially responsible companies as at least as profitable as conventional companies. Junkus and Berry (2010) find that socially responsible investors tend to be female, single, better educated and younger than conventional investors. However, socially responsible investors also tend to be less wealthy.

In general, these choices are not easy for individuals and might lead to inconsistent behavior (Apostolakis et al. 2018). It is not clear how much future losses individuals should be willing to accept to invest in medical innovation, better working conditions, or less pollution.

1.10   Financing institutions and instruments

Financing institutions are necessary to provide capital to social ventures. In general, it is possible to differentiate between social venture capital funds, social and ethical banks, crowdfunding platforms, and alternative institutions. Each of these institutions has a different risk–return profile.

Social venture capital funds apply the mechanisms of venture capital funds to the social sector. They usually invest in 10–20 enterprises and work closely with them to increase the value of their investment (Letts, Ryan, and Grossman 1997; Spiess-Knafl and Aschari-Lincoln 2015). They are organized in the European Venture Philanthropy Association (EVPA) or the Asian Venture Philanthropy Network (AVPN).

Social banks are providing debt capital to the impact sector and are only funding projects which have a social, local, or ecological value (Weber 2014). They either operate as social banking units in larger commercial banks or as independent entities. Globally, these banks are organized in various networks such as the Global Alliance on Banking for Values (GABV) or the European Federation of Ethical and Alternative Banks and Financiers (FEBEA).

Crowdfunding platforms are another form of financing institution. They pool investments from a crowd of individuals and use different forms of financing instruments. Some crowdfunding platforms provide equity capital to the fundraising companies. They are often referred to as crowdinvesting platforms. Usually, there is an entity which pools the investments and takes decisions on behalf of the crowd investors. Other crowdfunding platforms are providing loans to the fundraising companies. The fields can include microfinance, traditional consumer companies, or social real estate.

Some nonprofit organizations use their embeddedness in the civil society to collect donations via crowdfunding platforms. The last type of crowdfunding platforms offers rewards. Fans might pre-finance music recordings or films, or consumers buy a certain product which still needs to be developed.

The institutions discussed above provide different forms of financing instruments. The main financing instruments are equity and debt capital. Other forms are usually a combination of debt and equity capital. There are no limits on how to structure the financing instruments to accommodate the objectives of the capital providers. Examples include mezzanine capital, revenue share agreements, or recoverable grants. Mezzanine capital combines the repayment requirement of debt capital with some form of profit participation from equity capital.

Equity capital is the form of capital which gives investors a share of the company and control and voting rights. Equity capital is not repayable which means that investors need to find other parties if they want to exit their investment. Investors usually take a share of 5%–25% of the equity capital and negotiate detailed term sheets with the founders to outline actions in future scenarios.

Debt capital is usually provided by banks or loan funds. The company needs to repay the loan and pay in regular intervals interest payments. Debt capital offers more structuring options than equity capital. The sustainability-linked bonds are a large and growing market and a good example for the structuring flexibility.

In March and July 2021, Public Power Corp, a Greek power utility, has raised €1.150 billion with two bonds which link the interest payment to certain sustainability criteria. The first bond has raised €650 million with the condition that the company commits to reduce its CO_2 emissions by 40% at the end of 2022 compared to 2019. If the company fails to reduce its CO_2 emissions, the interest rate will increase by 50 basis points for the remaining duration of the bond. The first bond was six times oversubscribed (Sustainalytics 2021).

The second bond was even 6.5 times oversubscribed. It also linked interest payments to the reduction of CO_2 emissions. In the second bond, the commitment was a reduction of 57% by the end of 2023 compared to 2019. The power utility faces higher interest rates of 50 basis points if they fail to achieve this target (Sustainalytics 2021b).

The market for green and social bonds is another growing area. Companies and governments are issuing bonds where proceeds are earmarked for specific projects.

There are certain developments which facilitate this kind of products. For example, the United Kingdom introduced in 2011 a database which tracks the unit costs of hundreds of different social interventions (Greater Manchester Combined Authority 2022). It contains information on the costs of imprisonments, unemployment, or childcare.

In addition, new models link payments to certain social outcomes. Foundations and funds have been willing to innovate and try new financing schemes. Another example is revenue share agreements. Revenue share agreements are simple agreements in which the investor provides capital and receives a certain share of the revenues. A revenue share agreement gives the organization a variable cost structure, and it shares the risks between both parties.

1.11   General problems in the impact space

The wider social sector and the impact space in general are important for the daily lives of millions of people. Parents need to consider if they want to send their children to public school or church-run schools. Adults need to consider if they prefer commercial or nonprofit elderly home cares for their elderly parents.

Steinberg (2006) has introduced a model which shows how the market and the public authorities interact. Normally, all activities are run by the market. There is the invisible hand which makes sure that everyone can buy bread, cinema tickets, and lemonades.

However, the market does not always work as intended. If there is a market failure, public authorities can intervene with a range of policy actions such as regulation, mandates, or direct supply. If these policy actions do not lead to the intended results, there is room for the nonprofit sector.

Some argue that the nonprofit or the wider social sector exists to solve the trust problem. For example, it is almost impossible to assess the quality of kindergartens or elderly home cares. It might be the case that some use sedative medicaments to reduce the number of caring personnel. It is somehow obvious that the restriction

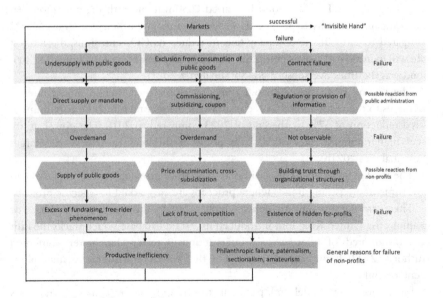

FIGURE 1.2 Three-failure model

Source: Steinberg (2006)

on profit distributions leads to a more trusted organization (e.g., Badelt 1997). Trust is one of the key currencies in the impact space. It is not easy to scale trust as perceived integrity is a key part for trustworthiness (Achleitner et al. 2013).

Nonprofit organizations can help to overcome the contract failure problem by building trust through its organizational structure. The blockchain technology is a technology which might help to overcome the trust problem in many instances.

In addition, nonprofit organizations are often able to charge different fees depending on the ability and capacity to pay clients, and these tend to comply with these moral standards. This would not be possible for commercial companies. Nonprofits are thus often able to deliver services as they have other means to organize and deliver.

Notes

1 For more information, see https://sdgs.un.org/goals
2 The number is based on 2007 dollars, with a discount rate of 3% for emissions in 2020.
3 Greenhouse gases include carbon dioxide, methane, nitrous oxide, and fluorinated gases. These gases are emitted through the burning of fossil fuel, deforestation, or agricultural practices.
4 For more information, see https://frutafeia.pt/
5 Some also refer to it as distributed ledger technology (DLT). Definitions can be found in Chapter 5.

2
INTRODUCTION TO ARTIFICIAL INTELLIGENCE

2.1 How to think about artificial intelligence

Artificial intelligence (AI) seems to be an omnipresent topic these days. Every day brings new use cases. Well-known use cases include the identification of hate speech at social media platforms, digital assistants for individuals, fraud detection at financial institutions, or the identification of cats and dogs in online videos.

There are different ways to think about AI. A few examples might be helpful to understand the opportunities, the main principles, as well as the limitations.

The first approach is to consider how input and output can be used to generate rules.

Traditionally, programmers write code to execute certain algorithm steps. A program which converts temperature in Fahrenheit would define two variables and conduct the multiplication and addition. These are relatively easy operations, but more complex calculations can quickly expand to thousands of lines of code. In other words, programmers write code which converts input data into output data with predefined rules.

Machine learning is different. It only needs the input data and the output data and derives the rules from these two datasets as illustrated below.[1]

Given that the rules are generated with the help of input and output, it is obvious that the data quality is of crucial importance. Supervised learning needs to work with labels which identify the outputs. Take the example of breast cancer diagnosis. If the underlying labels are of low quality, the results will also be of low quality and of little value in the clinical practice.

One of the most intuitive ways to understand the applications of AI is to use your smartphone. You might have thousands of pictures on your smartphone, and it might be cumbersome to search for certain images.

DOI: 10.4324/9781003218913-2

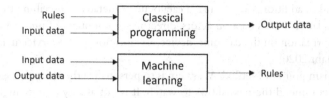

FIGURE 2.1 The difference between classical programming and machine learning

Source: Own illustration

(a)   (b)   (c)

FIGURE 2.2 Image search for "zebra"

Source: Own images

This is an example of a picture search using "zebra." The AI-based search algorithm does not miss a single picture of zebras and finds as well as pictures of zebra stripes.

Imagine that you want to write an algorithm that identifies zebras in thousands of images. It is hard to imagine someone writing an algorithm which can identify zebras in all instances. Once you have accomplished to identify zebras, it is almost impossible to replicate the code to use it for bears or donkeys.

The images above were identified in smartphone images using the system's neural network. It even works for texts and videos.

Another aspect is the sheer quantity of available data. Imagine the recommendation function at different platforms such as Spotify, Amazon, or Netflix. In principle, it is an approach to identify patterns of similar tastes and needs. There are often tens of millions of customers each with hundreds or thousands of data points. It would be almost impossible to come up with a manual classification scheme which keeps up with the latest developments in niche areas of the music or movie industry.

Netflix is a good example as it has access to plenty of data generated on the platform. The users rate shows, search shows, and start and stop streaming at certain points, and in addition, there is a rich catalogue of metadata describing the content. The metadata contains data on actors, directors, or countries of production. There is also information on the day, time, device, and location of the service usage (Iansiti and Lakhani 2020).

The main point of Netflix's AI system is to personalize the streaming experience and to recommend the next shows to watch. It is not as easy as one might expect. Multiple persons might share one account; users might want to see romantic as well as action movies. The selection of titles will also depend on the day of the week and the time of streaming. The streaming and traffic patterns are widely varying.

Netflix is personalizing almost every aspect of the start screen seen by users. In total, 80% of titles watched were recommended using, among others, personalized images of the titles or personalized descriptions. It is meant to help users find content they will likely watch. Netflix is also using it to decide on new content given the experiences of the past which content was successful (Netflix 2021).

The same aspects also apply to all other platforms recommending products, songs, or other content to their users. It would hardly be feasible without AI systems.

Another interesting aspect is the recognition of handwritten numbers. Humans spend a lot of time recognizing patterns. Character recognition is one such task which can save significant amounts of time for humans if implemented as a system.

The classification of handwritten numbers was one of the earlier examples. When it was commercially implemented at the end of the 1990s, the error rates for handwritten addresses were still as high as 60%–70% (Government Executive 1999). It improved dramatically to 1.5% in 2013 (Nixon 2013). This shows the steep improvements and learning curve for the algorithms.

FIGURE 2.3 Examples of handwritten numbers

Source: Github (2019)

The standard dataset is the MNIST database created by LeCun in 1998. It consists of 60,000 training and 10,000 testing images. The handwritten numbers above give an indication of the difficulties in automatically reading them. Pairs such as 1 and 7 can be easily confused, but there are other easily confused pairs such as 3 and 8 or 9 and 0.

These similarities explain why even the human error rate for classifying hand-written numbers is around 2% (Chaaban and Scheessele 2007). On the contrary, the error rate for classifying handwritten numbers is well below 1% for AI systems (LeCun, Cortes, and Burges 1998).

There are different types of techniques which have been implemented to read handwritten digits. The table shows how different techniques lead to different error rates (Baldominos, Saez, and Isasi 2019). The number of techniques might be overwhelming, but it is important to keep in mind that there are many different techniques used in this field.

This example is also a reminder of the implication for labor workforces. It saves hundreds of millions of US dollars for the US Postal Services and probably billions of US dollars for all postal services globally. Manually sorting letters and parcels is a repetitive and routine task, and there are surely many arguments to automatize these processes.

However, it is a typical job which is now mainly done by machines. It is also interesting to note how the accuracy improved radically over time. While at the beginning only a third of the mail was correctly classified, the accuracy now exceeds those of humans.

2.2 Introduction to data science

Computer science is different from other sciences. Computer scientists usually focus more on algorithms and less on the datasets they are using. In addition, in computer science, everything is either false or true. This is rarely the case in other scientific disciplines (Skiena 2017).

Data science is more like the other sciences in this regard. It is usually very complicated to construct datasets, and probabilistic approaches play an important role. Data science is also the search for insights based on data, and there are two different approaches (Skiena 2017).

The first approach is the hypothesis-driven paradigm. A research usually project starts with a hypothesis based on the literature. A hypothesis might be that an increase in the number of vaccinated people reduces the overall number of infections. The researcher would then search the relevant data and verify or falsify the hypoth-esis. The researcher will soon realize that it depends on the season, the number of infected persons, general mobility, and many other variables.

Another researcher might postulate that refugee children are more likely to become entrepreneurs as they are used to manage scarce resources. The researcher might then search data to verify or falsify the hypothesis. Data can include the biography of entrepreneurs, the growth as well as failure rate, and the year of the creation of the company or the industry.

TABLE 2.1 Comparison of the most competitive results for the recognition of handwritten numbers

Technique	Test Error Rate
NN 6-layer 5,700 hidden units	0.35%
MSRV C-SVDDNet	0.35%
Committee of 25 NN 2-layer 800 hidden units	0.39%
RNN	0.45%
K-NN (P2DHMDM)	0.52%
COSFIRE	0.52%
K-NN (IDM)	0.54%
Task-driven dictionary learning	0.54%
Virtual SVM, deg-9 poly, 2-pixel jit	0.56%
RF-C-ELM, 15,000 hidden units	0.57%
PCANet (LDANet-2)	0.62%
K-NN (shape context)	0.63%
Pooling + SVM	0.64%
Virtual SVM, deg-9 poly, 1-pixel jit	0.68%
NN 2-layer 800 hidden units, XE loss	0.70%
SOAE-s with sparse connectivity and activity	0.75%
SVM, deg-9 poly	0.80%
Product of stumps on Haar f.	0.87%
NN 2-layer 800 hidden units, MSE loss	0.90%
CNN (2 conv, 1 dense, relu) with DropConnect	0.21%
Committee of 25 CNNs	0.23%
CNN with APAC	0.23%
CNN (2 conv, 1 relu, relu) with dropout	0.27%
Committee of 7 CNNs	0.27%
Deep CNN	0.35%
CNN (2 conv, 1 dense), unsup pretraining	0.39%
CNN, XE loss	0.40%
Scattering convolution networks + SVM	0.43%
Feature Extractor + SVM	0.54%
CNN Boosted LeNet-4	0.70%
CNN LeNet-5	0.80%

Source: Baldominos, Saez, and Isasi (2019).

This might be a better approach for many research questions as it reduces the risks of random relationships. However, it might be easy to miss interesting observations.

The second approach is the data-driven paradigm which starts with a dataset and asks what kind of interesting questions can be addressed with it. This makes sense when there are too many variables to consider. Findings from this approach should always be taken with some caution as some effects might be purely random and nonreplicable in other contexts. However, these findings can be corroborated with further analyses.

There are two common problems which can be seen in this space. Models either try to classify or predict with a sample of data. The first common problem is the

TABLE 2.2 Schools of thought

	Symbolists	Connectionists	Evolutionaries	Bayesians	Analogizers
Representation	Logic	Neural networks	Genetic programs	Graphical models	Support vectors
Evaluation	Accuracy	Squared error	Fitness	Posterior probability	Margin
Optimization	Inverse deduction	Gradient descent	Genetic search	Probabilistic inference	Constrained optimization

Source: Domingos (2015).

classification or data points. You might want to know if an e-mail is spam or which documents share the same features. It can also be a problem of deciding on the genre of a certain book or movie. The second common problem is to predict the outcome with a set of input variables. This is usually done with regression analyses. For example, an insurance company has information regarding the weight, height, and education and wants to predict the life expectancy of its clients.

2.3   Historical development of AI

AI is a rather fluid field in the sense that methods and approaches are regularly changing. Each decade has its preferred tools and methods. In addition, there are different schools of thought. The architecture of the AI systems is also constantly changing.

Depending on the year of publication and the background of the author, AI will be differently explained and classified. A book published in the 1970s and 1980s might have emphasized expert networks, while a book published in 2020 will most likely focus on neural networks.

This also hints at the fact that over time there were different schools of thought. In each phase, different logics and schools of thought were dominant.

It is often a bit confusing to follow the discussion as authors often follow different definitions and perspectives. Nowadays, most focus on neural networks which have also received most of the available commercial and public funding. There are also other learning machines such as support vector machines or genetic programs. All of them have different representations, evaluations, and optimization methods. Domingos (2015) classifies the five different schools of thought according to their main representation, evaluation, and optimization.

Some such as Haenlein and Kaplan (2019) trace the history back to the short story *Runaround* by Asimov (1942) which states the Three Laws of Robotics:

(1) a robot may not injure a human being or, through inaction, allow a human being to come to harm; (2) a robot must obey the orders given to it by human beings except where such orders would conflict with the First

Law; and (3) a robot must protect its own existence as long as such protection does not conflict with the First or Second Laws.

The essay on "Computing Machinery and Intelligence" published by Turing in 1950 was also seen as a starting point. It introduced the Turing test of the imitation game to determine if a machine exhibits human-like intelligence.

However, histories of AI usually start with the Dartmouth conference which was a summer seminar organized by John McCarthy and took place in 1956. The key idea was to program machines which are able to learn for themselves.

In the proposal to the Rockefeller Foundation, the researchers have outlined the summer seminar in the following way (McCarthy et al. 1955):

> We propose that a 2-month, 10-man study of artificial intelligence be carried out during the summer of 1956 at Dartmouth College in Hanover, New Hampshire. The study is to proceed on the basis of the conjecture that every aspect of learning or any other feature of intelligence can in principle be so precisely described that a machine can be made to simulate it. An attempt will be made to find how to make machines use language, form abstractions and concepts, solve kinds of problems now reserved for humans, and improve themselves. We think that a significant advance can be made in one or more of these problems if a carefully selected group of scientists work on it together for a summer.

Russell and Norvig (2002) point out that already the objectives outlined in this proposal explain the need to create a separate field. There is the idea of duplicating creativity or language use as well as a very different methodology.

Some of the early programs included a Geometry Theorem Prover by Herbert Gelernter proving theorems, programs to play checkers by Arthur Samuel, and the Logic Theorist by Allen Newell and Herbert Simon.

Games are an especially suitable domain as there are strict rules and a limited environment. In addition, it is forbidden to invent new rules or enlarge the playing field. Outside of the games domain, the settings are less clear, and rules are constantly changing.

However, limited computing time and a lack of memory were major drawbacks which led, among others, to the first AI winter. Some of the initial assumptions did not work out as expected. For example, it was not sufficient to take grammatic rules and a dictionary to translate text. In addition, some of the early AI programs tried out different solutions until a solution was found. This worked perfectly fine in limited environments but did not work as expected at scale (Russell and Norvig 2020).

An often-cited example is a failure in translation. After the launch of Sputnik, the US National Research Council supported the translation of Russian scientific articles. However, these programs never were implemented successfully. A program was developed to translate from Russian into English. For testing purposes, sentences were translated from English into Russian and back into Russian. The sentence "The spirit is willing, but the flesh is weak" became "The vodka is good, but the meat is rotten." The phrase "out of sight, out of mind" became "invisible, insane" (Pollack 1983). In addition, Minsky and Papert (1969) wrote an influential book showing the limit of what simple neural networks could do.

Starting already in 1969, knowledge-based systems or expert systems became more popular. MYCIN was one such example. It contained about 450 rules to diagnose blood infections. The rules were acquired by interviewing doctors and other experts (Russell and Norvig 2020). These systems were started to be commercialized in the early 1980s. Although these approaches were later abandoned, there were some major success stories where companies saved significant amounts of money.

Some consider the 1990s as another AI winter. However, in 1997, IBM's Deep Blue beat Gary Kasparov. This hype was repeated in 2017 when AlphaGo beat the number one ranked player in Go. Researchers could build on decades of research on the properties of the models and save time developing and deploying. For example, in the mid-1980s, the idea of back-propagation was reinvented and helped to advance the field of the connectionists which were developing neural networks.

The 2000s saw three major trends which explain a turning point for the field (Fradkov 2020). The early 2000s marked the beginning of Big Data. Companies started to generate and store massive amounts of data. It became a necessity to adopt and experiment with new approaches. Google was a pioneer in reducing the costs of parallel computing. MapReduce and Hadoop enabled the company to distribute the processing of data between simple processors. In addition, the performance of Graphics Processing Unit (GPU) increased substantially. It was also the time when the research by Yann LeCun, Yoshua Bengio, and Geoffrey Hinton proved to be valuable. Deep neural networks were ready to be implemented, and enough research was already accumulated (Fradkov 2020).

The 2010s were the decade of neural networks. The current dominant form of neural networks was only widely deployed starting in the early 2010s. Neural networks started to outperform existing models such as Hidden Markov models significantly. One intern at Microsoft was able to outperform the existing model with a neural network he built on his own (Metz 2021).

The big-tech companies such as Microsoft and Google started investing in this technology and acquired start-ups in this space. Some noteworthy acquisitions were DNNresearch by Google in 2012 or DeedMind also by Google in 2014. Given the dominance of the big-tech companies, the field is still open source in nature, and costs for the implementation have decreased over the last years.

The current models are mostly trying to break down problems into smaller problems and solve them. This so-called narrow AI is used to solve relatively narrow or focused problems. It is used for recommendation on video platforms or robots choosing waste for recycling.

2.4 Diversity of approaches

AI-based applications have been successful playing games such as chess, GO, Jeopardy, or Poker. Games are good environments as there are clear rules and a large but limited number of options. This explains why games are often used to develop AI systems. In a non-games environment, there have been outstanding successes in areas such as speech or face recognition or medical imaging.

The deployment of AI has led to significant cost reductions in some areas. Translation is offered for free at various websites. Speech transcriptions cost less than $1 per hour with instantaneous results. This service used to be a lengthy and expensive process which involved bringing a tape to a local service provider. Social media companies implement AI-based tools to identify hate speech. Weapon manufacturers aim to use AI in battlefields.

Investments have been increasing substantially over the last years. It involved public funding, military spending, and private investments. Drivers have been the data ubiquity and the increase of cloud-based processing power.

Machine learning and AI as terms are used rather interchangeably. AI is the term which has first been used by McCarthy et al. (1955). It described a set of techniques to simulate human intelligence. Some of the early systems were rule-based or expert systems.

For example, the first program capable of playing checkers at a strong amateur level was basically a search tree assigning values for each branch of the tree (Samuel 1959). The paper already outlined the machine learning options, and the author is also credited with inventing the term. However, the program itself did not involve any actual learning.

Most of the early programs were symbolic or logic-based programs. For example, it is possible to formulate hundreds of different rules to classify medical images which would be a rule-based approach. These rule-based systems soon ran into troubles, and a solution was to let the algorithms learn with the data. Machine learning was the next step. Instead of specifying steps to solve a given problem, a learning algorithm would derive it from the data. Machine learning is a statistical approach to learn from data or experience. It uses statistical approaches to classify data and learn from them.

Most see machine learning as a subset of AI. One advantage of machine learning algorithms is the increase in quality when the sample of data increases. Most AI systems are nowadays based on machine learning (Bommasani et al. 2021).

Another category of AI system is summarized as deep learning. Whereas machine learning algorithms include a range of different techniques such as decision trees or Naïve Bayes, deep learning is based on artificial neural networks. These models can better handle the complexities of large datasets. The deep refers to the number of layers in artificial neural networks. Most of the industry's best-performing algorithms are deep learning algorithms.

The figure below illustrates how the computation paths developed over time. Linear regression models or decision list networks have rather shorter computation

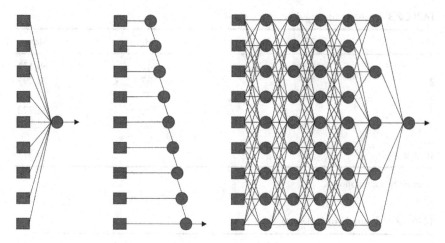

FIGURE 2.4 Development of models over time

Source: Russell and Norvig (2020)

paths. The advantage of neural networks is their longer and interdependent computation paths which enable better performance.

2.5 Data structure

The OECD (2019) has proposed a classification scheme for AI systems and takes a context-specific approach. It classifies the input and output data as well as the type of model and the objectives of the system.

Data are the necessary ingredient of all AI-based systems. There are complete fields of studies related to the analysis of data. For example, econometrics is the study of applying statistical tools to economic questions. It is not always necessary to have large datasets. Take the example of voter preferences where it is possible to analyze every newspaper article and tweet and still have less reliable results than relatively small-scale polls with 1,000 representative voters.

There are different types of data. One of the best studied economic phenomena is the effect of years of schooling on income. The following table is only meant to illustrate the relationship. There are thousands of persons, but only a few data points for each one. These data points might include the years of schooling, age or year of birth, and the annual income.

Economists would be interested in knowing more about the concrete relationship between schooling and learnings. Regression analyses can answer these questions and provide insights in how much different factors influence the final results.

In most cases, data are messy, and it is hard to determine which factors really drive outcomes. The following table might illustrate online click behavior, maintenance schedules for factories, or the school attendance and influencing factors.

TABLE 2.3 Example of long data

Person	Years of Schooling	Age	Income
1	12	47	50,131
2	15	37	78,797
3	11	27	73,409
4	10	36	37,723
5	9	30	48,488
...	...	...	...
10,000	11	59	55,371

Source: Own illustration.

TABLE 2.4 Example of wide data

User	Factor 1	Factor 2	Factor 3	Factor 4	Factor 5	Factor 6	Factor 7	...	Outcome
1	0	201	8	4	1	9	76	...	680
2	1	956	180	1	0	9	86	...	990
3	0	713	269	5	0	10	100	...	1,054
4	0	987	282	3	0	10	55	...	1,217
5	0	564	129	5	0	7	84	...	947
6	1	545	213	4	0	4	97	...	1,077
...	...	...	...	...	...	...	...	...	...
10,000	1	426	189	3	0	11	52	...	1,683

Source: Own illustration.

Artificial neural networks might be a tool to generate insights from these datasets. The problem remains that the models are not easily understandable.

There are also different types of data. Some data are continuous and real time, while other data are only uploaded once a month or in irregular patterns. There might also be static data such as the geographic size of countries or cities while the number of homeless people changes continuously.

Some data are structured, while other data are unstructured. Structured data usually means that there are labels for each variable. A spreadsheet or a relational database is always structured. Unstructured data come without labels. It can be audio files, images, or a collection of text from the internet. In many cases, images need to be labeled and manually sorted.

The data quality is of major concern. Typos, double entries, or faulty entries all reduce the quality of the dataset and lead to low-quality results.

2.6 Types of learning

The field of machine learning has its roots in learning how to adapt to new circumstances. In principle, a designer could just design a perfect program which would not need any improvements over time. This is tricky to achieve, and there are three main reasons why learning is relevant (Russell and Norvig 2020).

The first aspect is that it is impossible to imagine all possible scenarios and situations in the future. For example, an autonomous car might encounter new situations which the car needs to adapt to. The second aspect is that learning is necessary as contexts change over time. There are differences in share price movements which depend on many different factors. For example, it might make a difference if inflation is well above long-term averages or if geopolitical tensions are high. The third aspect is that it is sometimes difficult to come up with a good solution. Facial recognition or image recognition is one such example. It is fairly easy for humans to differentiate between dogs and cats, but it might be impossible to write 100 rules to differentiate between dogs and cats.

There are different approaches to how models can be learned. There are basically three different types of learning which are supervised learning, unsupervised learning, and reinforcement learning. They are different in how the model is being trained.

For supervised learning, the system is given the input and the output. The relationship between the input and the output is an unknown function which needs to be determined. The system will learn how to predict the outcomes. Examples are classification tasks.

A car salesperson might want to model the price of used cars and has access to a database containing previous sales prices together with the relevant features. It would be possible to build a model which predicts the market value of these cars. A teacher might be interested in modeling the attendance rates of students and their final marks.

Another supervised learning example is image recognition. A database might contain thousands of labelled pictures with dogs, cats, and cows which are used to train a neural network to detect these animals in pictures.

Examples are classification and regression. For classification, these models work well for fraud detection, image classification, or diagnostics. For regression, these are used for forecasting or predictions. A regression model is minimizing the empirical loss by finding values for the weights of this function:

$$y = w_1 x + w_0$$

The learning process involves regular adjustments of the weights minimizing the loss. Usually, it is referred to as the gradient descent approach. This approach can also be implemented with multivariate linear regression and is also the basis behind artificial neural networks.

The second group of learning algorithm is those using unsupervised learning. The system receives input and needs to cluster or group inputs together. There are cases where you do not know the answer and want to create a model which clusters the data. The model would cluster clients and data points in separate groups which is helpful to find new offers and generate additional insights. Examples include recommendation systems or customer segmentation. Unsupervised learning is also used for dimensionality reduction methods such as big data visualization or compression.

The third group of learning is based on reinforcement learning. Self-driving cars are often referred to as examples where the system receives feedback about its decisions. "Agents" operate in an environment where they need to perform certain activities. This environment can be roads for autonomous cars or video games. The agent receives points or scores for the way they operate in this environment. Reinforcement learning is used among others for robot navigation, games, or skill acquisitions.

It is necessary to train models with training data. These models should be tested with separate test data to avoid overfitting. Models can be assessed measuring the classification error. It states how many predictions were wrong and right. An error rate of 1% means that 99 out of 100 predictions were correct or 1 out of 100 predictions was wrong.

2.7 Definition of AI

The term 'artificial intelligence' was first coined by John McCarthy in 1956, and the concept has seen several boom-and-bust cycles since then. Deep learning was coined by Geoff Hinton in 2007 to describe neural networks.

The High-Level Expert Group on Artificial Intelligence (2019) defines AI in the following way:

> Artificial intelligence (AI) systems are software (and possibly also hardware) systems designed by humans that, given a complex goal, act in the physical or digital dimension by perceiving their environment through data acquisition, interpreting the collected structured or unstructured data, reasoning on the knowledge, or processing the information, derived from this data and deciding the best action(s) to take to achieve the given goal. AI systems can either use symbolic rules or learn a numeric model, and they can also adapt their behavior by analysing how the environment is affected by their previous actions.
>
> As a scientific discipline, AI includes several approaches and techniques, such as machine learning (of which deep learning and reinforcement learning are specific examples), machine reasoning (which includes planning, scheduling, knowledge representation and reasoning, search, and optimization), and robotics (which includes control, perception, sensors and actuators, as well as the integration of all other techniques into cyber-physical systems).

This definition highlights the diversity of approaches. The main definitional point is that AI systems process input data and suggest or take actions. Another definition has been introduced by the OECD's AI Expert Group (AIGO). It defines AI as

machine-based system that can, for a given set of human-defined objectives, make predictions, recommendations or decisions influencing real or virtual environments. It uses machine and/or human-based inputs to perceive
real and/or virtual environments; abstract such perceptions into models (in
an automated manner e.g. with ML or manually); and use model inference
to formulate options for information or action. AI systems are designed to
operate with varying levels of autonomy.

This definition highlights that AI systems are predicting, recommending, or
deciding. Input data are fed into models which either inform the user or are taking
action themselves.

2.8 Mechanics of neural networks

Most of the work in the field is now focused on developing neural networks. These
neural networks consist of at least three layers. There is one input layer, one or multiple hidden layers, and one output layer. The figure below illustrates the structure
of such neural networks.

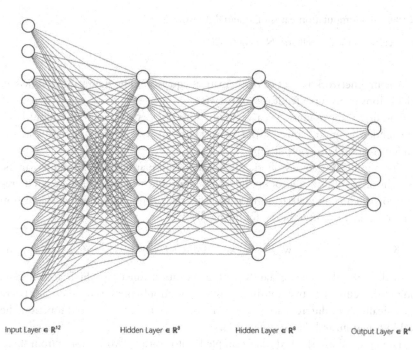

Input Layer ∈ R^{12} Hidden Layer ∈ R^8 Hidden Layer ∈ R^8 Output Layer ∈ R^4

FIGURE 2.5 Structure of a neural network with two hidden layers

Source: Lenail (2022)

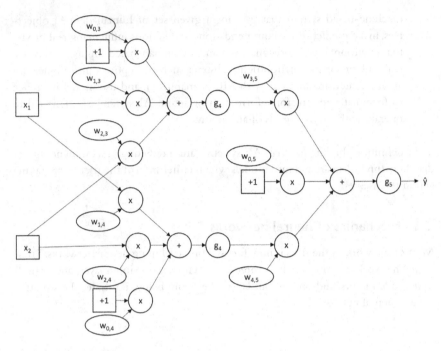

FIGURE 2.6 Computation paths of a neural network

Source: Based on Russell and Norvig (2020)

A neural network is a set of mathematical equations. The figure above shows all calculations in a simple feedforward network.

The figure above illustrates a very simple neural network with one input layer, one hidden layer, and one output layer. There are two inputs, two units in the hidden layer, and one output unit.

The figure also shows all the necessary computations. The weights can be thought of as volume control knobs which control how important the related predecessor is. The complete formula is basically the sum of all individual calculation steps and can be written in the following form:

$$\hat{y} = g_5(w_{0,5} + w_{3,5}\, g_3(w_{0,3} + w_{1,3}\, x_1 + w_{2,3}\, x_2) + w_{4,5}\, g_4(w_{0,4} + w_{1,4}\, x_1 + w_{2,4}\, x_2)).$$

In the formula above, g stands for the activation function which activates the individual neurons. Activation functions are commonly nonlinear functions. There are basically three different activation functions which are the sigmoid function, the ReLU function, and the tanh function.

The figure above showed a very simple feedforward network. Going from there, all kinds of different models have been developed in the last decades. Networks differ in terms of their form. That means how many hidden layers or input units are used. There are also differences in the way the calculations are structured.

A recurrent network is a network which feeds outputs back into the network. This forms a dynamical system which work well for text and audio signals.

Convolutional neural networks (CNNs) are mainly used for image processing. There are certain patterns in how early layers are connected. Generative adversarial networks (GANs) consist of two networks, where one network is generating images, while the other network is separating generated from real images. Well-known examples are computer-generated paintings in the style of Picasso or Rembrandt.

The following table shows an overview of the different machine learning algorithms. It usually depends on the learning tasks. Classification or regressions tasks need other algorithms than clustering or robotics.

TABLE 2.5 Overview of machine learning algorithms

Supervised Learning	Unsupervised Learning	Reinforcement Learning
Learning task		
Classification and regression	Clustering and dimensionality reduction	Model-free and model-based
Most widely used machine learning algorithms		
Linear regression	k-means clustering	Q-learning
Logistical regression	t-Distributed stochastic	Temporal difference
Random forest	neighbor embedding	Monte-Carlo tree search
Gradient boosted trees	(t-SNE)	Asynchronous actor-
Support vector machines	Principal component	critic agents
Neural networks	analysis (PCA)	Deep Q-learning
Decision trees	Association rule	Temporal difference
Naïve Bayes	Instance-based	Dataset aggregation
Nearest neighbor	learning models	
	Artificial neural networks	
	Genetic algorithm	
	Deep learning models	

Source: Based on Nti et al. (2021).

TABLE 2.6 Ranking of machine learning methods

Method	Power of Expression	Ease of Interpretation	Ease of Use	Training Speed	Prediction Speed
Linear regression	5	9	9	9	9
Nearest neighbor	5	9	8	10	2
Naïve Bayes	4	8	7	9	8
Decision trees	8	8	7	7	9
Support vector machines	8	6	6	7	7
Boosting	9	6	6	6	6
Graphical models	9	8	3	4	4
Deep learning	10	3	4	3	7

Source: Skiena (2017).

Each algorithm has its advantages, and none performs well in each dimension. Skiena (2017) ranks the different machine learnings for their power of expression, ease of interpretation, ease of use, training speed, and prediction speed.

2.9 Ethical considerations and shortcomings

Companies developing machine learning rarely spend time to consider the ramifications and implications of their actions. There are many ethical concerns which should be addressed in this area (Mittelstadt et al. 2016). Algorithms have been found to be problematic in a range of industries such as bank loans, court judgments, predictive policing, or the evaluation of teacher performances (O'Neil 2016). There was also widespread resistance against the use of algorithms in labor market agencies.

In general, the literature and discussions center around a few key areas.

One of the key ethical concerns is focused on the unfiltered and problematic datasets. Birhane, Prabhu, and Kahembwe (2021) analyze one of the largest datasets for AI purposes which is run by California-based nonprofit organizations. It contains 400 million samples of image–text pairs such as "blue cats."[2]

After searching through the dataset, they found that it only *risked amplifying hyper-sexualized and misogynist representation of women, but also presented results that were reminiscent of Anglo-centric, Euro-centric, and potentially, White-supremacist ideologies.* Even when datasets are retracted, they remain widely available as they have already been used to train models. Data are sold, merged, and used in derivative forms. The users have no control over how the data are being used.

Zou and Schiebinger (2018) point out that a major issue is the construction of the datasets on which the systems are trained. The images are often from US-centric databases which tend to underrepresent darker-skinned persons.

ImageNet is a major database for the training of AI systems (Russakovsky et al. 2015). Having common data-sets save a lot of efforts for the researchers, but they can also lead to biases if there are biases in the data. For ImageNet, Shankar et al. (2017) find that almost half of the images are coming from three countries which are the United States (32%), Great Britain (13%), and France (4%). Although these countries only account for a fraction of the global population, they contribute half of all images.

Another ethical concern is the lack of algorithmic accountability which means that AI systems are almost always a black box for the general public. The general public does not have access to the training data and also to the neural network itself. There is an understandable resistance to provide access to these systems which are often at the core of the company's operations. The problem of a black box is also that the old saying "Garbage in, garbage out" applies as well. In addition, these models are not interpretable for humans.

Although deep learning models or neural networks might perform better, some analysts prefer regression models as the most powerful features can be easily identified. There is thus a trade-off between an understanding of the data and the performance of the system.

AI systems also reproduce biases and structural disadvantages for certain groups. In a famous study, Buolamwini and Gebru (2018) evaluate commercial AI-gender classification systems. A first problem is that the training data contain on average around 80% of lighter-skinned persons. They also find that these commercial gender classification systems have error rates of up to 34.7% for darker-skinned women, while the error rate for light-skinned men is 0.8%.

Bender et al. (2021) show that large language models are not necessarily diverse in its results. It has to do with the persons contributing to content on the internet as one factor. Translation using AI system is reflecting inequalities and biases in society.

The tables below show the limits and gender biases in automatic translation. There is a tendency to identify better paying jobs with males and caring professions with females. The sentences below are Hungarian and Malay. Although there is no indication of gender in the sentences below, the automatic translation identifies men with managers and intelligences and women with caring professions and beauty. It is easy to understand the reasoning of the AI system, but it is also obvious that these translations help to preserve stereotypes.

Researchers have tested the translations in 12 gender-neutral languages and have found that the translations do not reproduce the real-world distribution. In reality, the female representation in certain occupations is much higher than in the translated sentences (Prates, Avelar, and Lamb 2020).

Misclassifications and errors can also often be found. In 2015, a Black software designer tweeted that Google's image recognition software was misclassifying him and a black female friend as gorillas. Understandably, the tweet caused a public relations (PR) disaster for Google, and the company blocked image searches for gorillas, monkeys, chimps, and chimpanzees since then. The same error happened at Facebook in 2021. Users who were watching a video featuring Black men were

TABLE 2.7 Translation of gender-neutral sentences

Original gender-neutral sentence	Translated sentences
ő vigyáz a gyerekekre.	she takes care of the kids.
ő egy menedzser.	he is a manager.
ő szép.	she is beautiful.
ő okos.	he is clever.
ő takarítja a házat.	she cleans the house.
ő egy mérnök.	he is an engineer.
dia menjaga anak-anak.	she takes care of the children.
dia seorang pengurus.	he is a manager.
dia cantik.	she's beautiful.
dia pandai.	She is smart.
dia mengemas rumah.	she's tidying up the house.
dia seorang jurutera.	he is an engineer.

Source: Own illustration.

asked if they wanted to watch more "videos about primates" (Jones 2021). This points toward the implications of errors and the difficulties of the technology.

The introduction above has shown how important training data are for the development of the AI systems. However, for users, it is usually impossible to keep track of their own data and reclaim them later.

Users have many devices which are actively collecting data and intruding into their privacy. Véliz (2020) is illustrating the typical daily routine which involves web searches, digital assistents, loyalty programs, house control, car management systems, and so on. All of these devices and programs are potentially problematic and have been found to violate the privacy of its users.

Even anonymous data can often be linked to certain persons. A famous example is the de-anonymization of the Netflix Prize dataset. Netflix has shared the anonymous movie rating of 500,000 individuals. Narayanan and Shmatikov (2008) have used the Internet Movie Database to successfully de-anonymize users from the dataset. Their results are impressive as "8 movie ratings (of which 2 may be completely wrong) and dates that may have a 14-day error, 99% of records can be uniquely identified in the dataset. For 68%, two ratings and dates (with a 3-day error) are sufficient." This has important implications as the de-anonymization might reveal political or sexual preferences.

Other issues include data glitches. For example, autonomous weapon systems operate on data that are often faulty. Disinformation is another concern (Buchanan et al. 2021) or the energy needs of language models (Bender et al. 2021).

There are many instances where public data are being transferred to private companies. In this context, the data-sharing agreement between the Royal Free Hospital and a Google's AI subsidiary, DeepMind, is often discussed. DeepMind received access to five years of patient data to predict acute kidney injuries. The results would then inform the development of an app to provide information about a patient situation. The data-sharing agreement raised concerns as patients might not be willing to share sensitive health data with a Google subsidiary (Hawkes 2016). It was later found that the data were shared on an inappropriate basis although the effectiveness of the app was confirmed (Iacobucci 2017).

This illustrates the tensions between the need to have good data to develop useful products and the trust which is needed in this area. Later, when DeepMind's health team joined Google Health, researchers pointed out that there is a need to address the deficit of trust to unlock the opportunities of the technology (Morley, Taddeo, and Floridi 2019).

There are also other instances. For example, webcrawlers collect information from the internet to use it for all kinds of different purposes. Nobody asks the creators and writers if they do consent in having their work used for whatever purpose.

One of the last concerns is about the impact of AI on job losses and potentially higher rates of unemployment. Automation was always feared to lead to large-scale job destruction, but people are working as much as ever. Automation is often argued to contribute to job losses and higher rates of unemployment. There are different perspectives on how automation and labor productivity impact employment and wages.

Notes

1 The difference between artificial intelligence and machine learning is explained in more detail below. Machine learning means that the system observes some data and derives hypotheses from these observations. This model is then used to take actions or give recommendations to the users. Artificial intelligence methods which do not rely on machine learning are mostly handcrafted knowledge systems. Expert systems which relied on human-crafted rules were popular until the 1980s.
2 For more information, see https://laion.ai/laion-400-open-dataset/

3

AI-FIRST IMPACT BUSINESS MODELS

3.1 Introduction

Chapter 2 has shown the underlying mechanisms of AI. This chapter will focus on the artificial intelligence (AI) factories and the business models which build systems based on AI. It includes aspects such as data management, methods, and business models which create impact for society.

There have been many discussions on which industries will become obsolete or at least disrupted. In the legal sector, much of the negotiations and the court-related activities will stay a human activity for the foreseeable future. However, law firms often have to read through thousands of pages which tends to be repetitive. This document analysis can be done with the help of AI systems. For example, one company might acquire another company which rents apartments to individuals. There might be 50,000 contracts which have a similar structure, and AI systems could flag those contracts a lawyer should read carefully. There are already examples where judges are relying on scores generated by AI systems to predict the likelihood that individuals will reoffend in the near term.

In the engineering area, most of the developments are related to the detection of faults in materials or to the prediction when machines will likely fail. In retail, much of the AI-based developments are related to customer preferences and generating insights for planning purposes. For transport and utilities, much of the interest is about predicting the future demand. It is very helpful for mobility companies or electricity demand at which times customers will require their services.

The following table shows examples of applications which can be observed in different sectors.

The list of use cases has already shown the range of business functions and users. Some systems are designed for consumers who might not even be aware of the underlying technology. Others are designed for professional users who can also interpret results.

DOI: 10.4324/9781003218913-3

TABLE 3.1 Uses of AI

Sector	Examples of applications	Source
Law and compliance	Document review and screening, pattern detection, calculation of the risk to reoffend, predictive policing, legal search, document generation, prediction of case outcomes	Alarie, Niblett, and Yoon (2018); Surden (2019)
Engineering and manufacturing	Fault diagnostics, robotics, anomaly detection and predictive maintenance, machine vision, wear and tear monitoring	Nti et al. (2021)
Retail	Warehouse robotics, customer insights and demand planning, inventory management, image recognition, customer preferences, personalization	Guha et al. (2021); Oosthuizen et al. (2021)
Transport	Predicting traffic patterns, flight route optimization, pricing models based on expected demand, self-driving cars, smart city	Abduljabbar et al. (2019)
Utilities	Electricity demand forecasting, predicting renewable energy generation	Kumar and Kalavathi (2018); Bedi and Toshniwal (2019)

Source: Own illustration.

3.2 The AI factory

Much of the recent hype was around the efficiency of AI-based companies. AI helps companies to increase their output without necessarily increasing the workforce. The efficiency usually depends on whether companies follow an AI-first approach or use AI to enhance existing processes.

There are various sources of data, and it is usually one of the hardest tasks to have access to data. A start-up might have new insights to identify cancerous cells at an early stage. The development of the model requires hundreds or thousands of images of specific cancerous cells for training purposes. The model needs to be fed with labeled images to build a classification model. In practice, this is rather complicated. Hospitals often do not have the data ready to share. There might be privacy issues. Sometimes, it is also an issue of different image sizes which might distort the final model.

Each AI system follows a lifecycle (Hapke and Nelson 2020). The first step is focused on data collection. The data need to be transformed in a format which the following components can work with. In the following step, the data need to be validated and preprocessed for training runs. The model training is a key part of the development as the system is trained to predict a certain output with the lowest error. The analysis for the model performance centers around accuracy, error rates, or consistency checks. After deployment, it needs to be monitored to identify potential issues, and there might be opportunities to capture new training data.

A social enterprise might be interested in building a model which can identify people at risk of homelessness. This might improve the allocation of resources and targeting of clients. A model might be relatively easy to develop, but they would need access to income data, personal background, and other sensitive data. It is hard to imagine that any public authority or individual would share this kind of data.

The Covid-19 pandemic has shown how difficult it can be to collect data consistently and globally. Some countries published their data in a machine-readable way, while other countries held press conferences streamed via social media to announce certain numbers. Access to data will remain one of the key barriers of the sector.

There is a lot of evidence showing that many datasets have been used beyond their original purposes and not in line with the expectations of the individuals. This will also remain a key challenge for the sector to ensure that data are handled with respect to the privacy of the individuals. The social sector has especially sensitive data. It might contain health data, unemployment data, personality assessments, poverty data, or the records of a food bank.

Some governments are actively promoting open data and are sharing the datasets they have. The United Kingdom has started a Unit Cost Database in 2011 which provides data for the costs of providing services. The costs for voluntary and private sector care homes for children might serve as an example.

Some countries have relatively strict access criteria which are sometimes restricted to academic research. The decision to grant access is again a trade-off between privacy concerns and research in the public interest. Some academic journals now require academics to share their data-sets when they publish papers.

There are also collections of datasets online. Kaggle is the most widely known platform for public datasets. As of January 2022, there are 50,000 public datasets

TABLE 3.2 Unit costs for voluntary and private sector care homes for children

Costs and Unit Estimation	2020/2021 Value
Capital costs (A and B)	£148 per resident week
A. Buildings	
B. Land	£31 per resident week
C. Total expenditure (minus capital)	£4,153 per resident week
D. Overheads	–
E. Other costs external services	£13.68 per resident week for school support
£4,332 establishment costs per resident week (includes A–C); £619 establishment costs per resident day (includes A–C). £4,345 per resident week (includes A–E); £621 per resident day (includes A–E).	

Source: Jones and Burns (2021).

which can be downloaded free of charge. However, it is rather unlikely that the specific dataset of interest will be on the platform.[1]

Some companies provide access to the data they are collecting. There might be various reasons for this. For example, Google is sharing some of its data freely to promote its platform. Others might see the public benefit or the limited costs of sharing their data.

In general, almost all data collected by private companies remains inaccessible for third parties. Some private companies are selling access to their data for relatively high prices. Costs usually start at a few thousand dollars.

Some organizations have their own data collection operations. If the data are not readily available, the remaining option is to construct the necessary datasets. This is usually referred to as scraping. In this process, information from websites is collected and used for their own commercial purposes. This can be problematic as some see it as intellectual property theft (Black 2016).

A common example is services for Amazon or Ebay. Third-party sellers are interested in the dynamics of the platform and can buy data from companies which monitor transactions, price developments, and comments. Another option is to use platforms which offer crowd support in generating data and often labels. These platforms are very efficient to quickly outsource small tasks. However, these tasks should be clearly specified and should not require advanced training (Skiena 2017).

The following answers are derived from a project which asks beneficiaries to answer questions about impact created by companies. The question was

> Name one company which impacts your life. We are interested in knowing which companies impact your daily life. Consider which company impacts your life positively or negatively. One name and one sentence are sufficient.

TABLE 3.3 Use of crowdsourcing for collecting input

Answer 1	The NIKE company has had a positive impact on my life since I was a child, because it is a very important multinational company, which cares about the right design to satisfy all users of different ages, with its beautiful durable designs and affordable prices.
Answer 2	King Soopers affects my life daily. I purchase fresh fruit and vegetables as well as non-food products. Almost everything I touch and need daily is satisfied at the grocery.
Answer 3	Apple: We are an apple family and use a lot of apple products. So due to that apple plays a huge role in our daily lives.
Answer 4	Google: Google makes a pretty big impact on my life every day. My email and daily calendar are set up through Google and that's basically how I organize most of my life.
Answer 5	Amazon: This company is best impact in my daily life, lot of thinks I easily get for this Amazon company. Walmart: Partnerships with centers of excellence of quality care, No-cost counseling session. Apple: $750 per year contributed for employer.

(continued)

TABLE 3.3 (Cont.)

Answer 6	Honda: I drive a Honda Accord almost daily and absolutely love using it. It's reliable, enjoyable to drive, and, above all, exceedingly safe.
Answer 7	CVS is important to me because they give me access to affordable prescriptions and vaccinations.
Answer 8	Amazon: The way of disrupting the people Amazon has created economic ripple effects that go far beyond the customer's wallet. Amazon, directly and indirectly, impacts inflation, jobs, and investment.
Answer 9	Facebook: it allows for easy tracking and updating of friends. Perfect for finding out what everyone is doing out there in the fun world.
Answer 10	Amazon has saved me countless trips to the stores and offers convenient returns.
Answer 11	Amazon is a company that impacts my daily life in a positive way. I save a lot of time shopping in this site, and plus there is MTurk which allows me to earn extra money each month.
Answer 12	Walmart company: Work provides the opportunity to meet new people and connect with others. The interaction that occurs between employees can result in a number of factors that have a positive impact on me, including trust and social support.
Answer 13	WinCo foods: A grocery store chain mostly in the west/northwest of the United States; I love this company. My grocery bill is usually a good 20%–30% lower than the other chain supermarkets in the area, plus the one I shop at is in easy walking distance from my home.
Answer 14	Apple: Due to the amount of devices, I have in my home. It is my primary technology that I use daily, and it usually helps make my life easier due to being part of the ecosystem.
Answer 15	Microsoft and their products like Office 360 have greatly helped with the current development in my work and my partners work and in the past with our studies greatly.
Answer 16	ICPC Bank asks me if I have a lot of money in life to earn more interest. Buying this bank housing loan is the biggest mistake for me. This is a Chinese company I do not know when buying a loan. I bought a loan without inquiring into this paragraph. I will suffer for the rest of my life with this bank loan.
Answer 17	Amazon is the company that has the biggest impact on my life because it helps in providing me an extra source of income I could not live without, as well as a place to buy things online. Amazon Mechanical Turk impacts my life everyday in a positive way by providing work for me to do for money.
Answer 18	Nestle: They own so many products that even if you go out of your way to avoid them you might buy from a subsidiary.
Answer 19	Patagonia impacts my life positively. They contribute to causes I care about, like protecting the environment, and they make high-quality clothing that are comfortable and functional in my everyday life.
Answer 20	Instagram is a company that impacts my daily life. It impacts it in a very positive way because it allows me to connect with people all over the world.

Source: Own illustration.

The examples show the potential and the limits of the approach. The examples include well-known consumer brands. Other approaches include gamification or captchas. Captchas are a tool to prove that users are indeed human by identifying cars and planes in images and thus help to train neural networks.

The advantage of AI systems is that it can easily include new data in the model. In a certain way, that is the main advantage of learning models discussed above. Data can take any form such as images, text, or numbers. This has not been feasible until a few years ago.

It is also interesting as these new alternative data have only been available for governments and secret services until a few years ago. Among these new data sources are drone data, satellite data, and ocean data. All these data sources can also be used for impact purposes.

Drones are an interesting new technology to discuss as they have negative and positive use cases. Among the rather negative use cases is the use of combat drones as unmanned combat aerial vehicles (UCAVs). During the Covid-19 pandemic, drones were also used for crowd surveillance and were even equipped with speakers to enforce lockdowns and ensure compliance with local guidelines (Chamola et al. 2020). Not all might enjoy receiving commands from unmanned drones.

However, there are also more positive use cases where drones are used to deliver medicines or to inspect solar panels, wind turbines, or crop areas. Drone data can be used to identify flooded areas or to understand the impact of natural disasters in the field. In addition, drones can produce higher resolution images than satellites and can also be used on cloudy days. The costs are relatively limited.

The problem with drones is the amount of footage they produce. A short flight might generate hundreds of high-resolution images which need to be assessed and analyzed. This quickly becomes a big data problem.

Access to satellite data used to be the privilege for governments, militaries, and secret services. Nowadays, satellite data can be accessible quite broadly and at low costs. The achievements are quite impressive. For example, Graesser et al. (2012) use satellite data and machine learning algorithms to identify formal and informal settlements in La Paz, Caracas, Kabul, and Kandahar.

To illustrate the almost limitless potential and scope of data, buoys are a good example. They can be used to measure wind, waves, and temperatures.

California-based Saildrone has raised $190 million until early 2022 to develop and expand a fleet of autonomous surface vehicles. These vehicles are powered by wind and solar and collect a range of data on fish populations, air–sea exchange of heat and carbon dioxide, and other ocean-related data.[2]

Sofar Ocean is another California-based start-up collecting ocean data which has raised $46 million from venture-capital funds so far. They have been placing more than 1,000 buoys in oceans which can collect air and sea surface temperature, wind speed, wind direction, and wave data, among others (Raghukumar et al. 2019). This kind of data is relevant for researchers and shipping companies trying to reduce the travel time of ships and thereby reducing greenhouse gas emissions.

One of the first steps in the data factory is the cleaning of the data. There is the saying that "garbage in, garbage out" which implies that low-quality data inevitably lead to low-quality results.

This is relatively easy to understand. Imagine the case of cancerous cells. If there are errors in the classification of malignant and benign cells, these errors are also part of the model as it was trained on the erroneous data.

There are also other kinds of problems. Some users might use unknown characters from other alphabets. Outliers might distort results. There might be issues in the data collection. Datasets might change over time. Sometimes, a new category is introduced, and datasets are not consistent anymore.

Data cleaning involves all sorts of aspects. Companies might have revenues in Bulgarian Lev and British pounds. It might be necessary to use exchange rates to have a common currency for all data. Data formats might be different for European and American datasets. Names might be written differently in different languages. For example, the last leader of the Soviet Union is written Gorbatschow in German, Gorbačëv in Italian, Gorbachev in English, and Gorbatchev in French.

A common problem arises when data are entered manually. There might be typos or other unusable data. Some companies use crowdsourcing platforms to check the accuracy of data. If both individuals enter the same data, it is accepted as correct.

3.3 Use of data

The operating model which dominated in the past was the analytical approach. Companies were gathering data and used the data to improve its operations. For example, hospital managers could use data to identify bottlenecks in the flow of patients. Waiting times are a good indicator to see where improvements can be made.

The new data-driven approach changes this approach. Data are at the core of the business and operating model. For example, Amazon can use the insights from other customers to suggest additional products. Spotify can construct playlists based

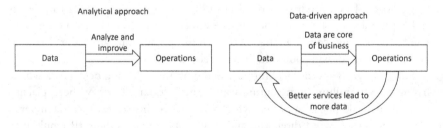

FIGURE 3.1 Use of data for the development of an AI-based business model

Source: Own illustration based on Iansiti and Lakhani (2020)

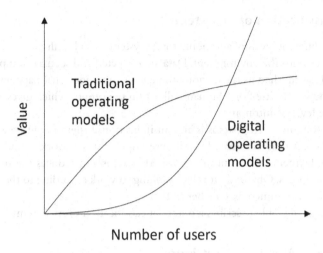

FIGURE 3.2 Different operating models

Source: Iansiti and Lakhani (2020)

on preferences of clients with similar music tastes. These business models would not be possible without access to data.

The value and strong economics of this model are based on the observation that each additional customer improves the operating model. Traditional manufacturing companies or hotel chains have natural limits to their economies of scale. This is different for AI-based companies as each additional customer helps to improve the accuracy of the data model and the underlying assumptions. For example, a company screening medical images can use the additional images to improve the AI system. A retail platform can improve the accuracy of its recommendations with a higher number of customers. The following figure shows this relationship.

The different paths also necessitate alternative growth strategies as there is a need to bridge the time until enough clients use this system (Chen 2021).

AI systems require a different approach as the datasets are much larger. While researchers might be able to use a spreadsheet and statistical tools to analyze their data, millions of data points are too large for traditional approaches. AI models are widely available off the shelf. The challenge remains to build a pipeline for the data flow. The data can come from governments, clients, or third parties. Each data source has its own interface. It is necessary to understand the data structure, the content, and how data are changed. For example, inflation or economic growth data are regularly revised which requires a constant reconciliation of the dataset.

Data need to be transformed so that it can be stored in databases, data warehouses, or data lakes. The data are then processed on data science platforms and finally displayed in some form of app, dashboard, or visualization (e.g., Hapke and Nelson 2020; Densmore 2021). The following figure shows how a modern data infrastructure is organized.

3.4 Classification of AI systems

There are different levels of autonomy for AI systems which influence the design of the interface with the environment. Data are collected and seen as an input. When the model has finished its calculations, there is the question what happens with the output. The system itself or a human will act on the output which gives an indication of the level of autonomy.

The autonomy of AI systems is also an indication if there might be a potential for job losses. A fully automated warehouse might displace workers and put them out of employment. More autonomy for AI systems also reduces the meaning of jobs for employees. Obviously, it is less fulfilling to work according to the schedules of a machine as outlined by Graeber (2019).

The following table describes a potential classification of AI systems.

3.5 Use of AI in public settings

The use of AI in public settings is one of the most discussed topics. It is a discussion involving human rights, legal frameworks, political preferences, and business opportunities. In general, it is a discussion about automated decision-making and algorithmic accountability.

Disaster risk management is an example where AI is relatively uncontested (Deparday et al. 2019). However, Take the example of facial recognition. It is convenient to save some time at the airport, but it is less convenient if citizens are tracked across public spaces.

The facial-recognition network in Moscow is a good example. It was supposed to help enforce quarantine restrictions or help to identify wanted persons in the streets. However, it was soon used to identify individuals protesting against President Vladimir Putin (Arkhipov and Rudnitsky 2021). The Chinese social scoring system is also seen as critical in this context.

It was also widely reported that the Taliban gained limited access to biometric data collected by the US military in Afghanistan. It is useful to collect biometric data for controlling and managing access to certain areas, but it also put those at risk who were working for the US military. Even sensitive relational data such as relationship and names of fathers and uncles might be a risk in the wrong hands (Guo and Noori 2021).

Many countries and cities are now banning facial recognition, and big-tech companies have been under pressure from their employees to stop providing these facial-recognition services.

It has also been seen critically that even supermarkets are using surveillance technology. For example, a Spanish supermarket was fined €2.5 million for illegally using facial-recognition technology. A Dutch supermarket chain also had to stop using a facial-recognition technology. The supermarket chain claimed that it wanted to protect its customers and prevent shoplifting.

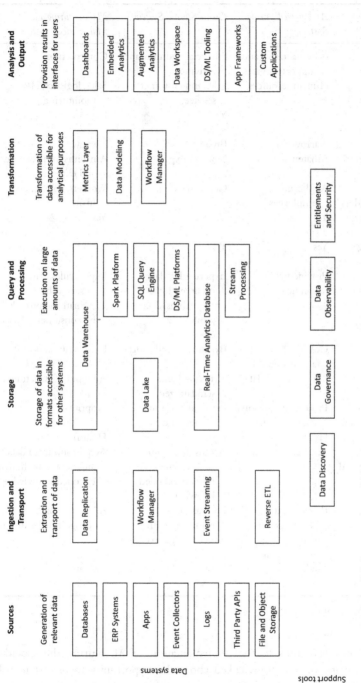

FIGURE 3.3 Multimodal data processing blueprint

Source: Bornstein, Casado, and Li (2020)

TABLE 3.4 Classification of AI systems

	AI-Powered Hiring Systems	Credit Scoring Systems	Manufacturing Plant Management System
Sector	Administrative and support services	Financial and insurance activities	Construction
Business function	Human resources	Sales and customer service	Sales, logistics, HR, monitoring
Critical function	No	Yes	No
Scale	Narrow	Broad	Narrow
System users	Amateurs	Non-AI expert	Amateurs, non-experts and experts
Impact stakeholders	Applicants/ employees	Consumers	Workers, consumers, firms
Human rights impact	Yes	Ye	Yes
Well-being impact	Yes	Yes	Yes
Data provenance	Provided by candidate	Expert rules, data observed by algorithms, data provided by consumer	Expert rules, data observed by algorithms, provided by consumers, derived
Collection	Collected by automated tools	By humans and tools	By humans and tools
Structure	Unstructured data	Structured and standardized	All types of structures
Rights and identifiability	Proprietary personal data, identified	Personal, proprietary, identified data	Proprietary
Model type	Hybrid	Hybrid	Hybrid
Model-building and training	Semi-supervised	Acquisition from data, augmented by human-encoded knowledge	Acquisition from data, augmented by human-encoded knowledge
Task	Personalization, interaction support, recognition	Forecasting and reasoning with knowledge structures	All (forecasting, recognition, reasoning)
Autonomy level	Medium	Low	Medium

Source: Based on OECD (2022a).

There are also limits to the implementation of AI. During the Covid-19 pandemic, many organizations talked about the opportunity to use AI to solve some of the problems. None of these opportunities were eventually realized and implemented.

The Covid-19 pandemic has shown the shortcomings when it comes to data management and contract tracing. The best data source is a small nonprofit organisation based in Oxford (World in Data) which has outperformed all public and private organizations.

The work with public data will remain one of the bigger issues in the coming years. There are already initiatives underway which aim to limit and regulate the use of data. One interesting idea is the publication of AI registers.

For example, Helsinki is publishing all AI systems in a separate register.[3] Helsinki is implementing data-based services to the inhabitants of the city. This is also sometimes referred to as a "smart city."

As of January 2022, the City of Helsinki is using AI systems for five different services. A parking chatbot answers questions related to the parking spots and costs in the city. Interestingly, residents and visitors can also claim a compensation if the AI system has provided them with a wrong information. There are two other chatbots to answer questions related to social services and healthcare.

Two AI systems are related to the operation of the Central Library. One system is basically a recommendation engine for the users. Another AI system aims to distribute books intelligently across the different branches of the library system. All branches of the Central Library share one large collection of 1.8 million books, and the AI system recommends which books should be stored in which branches. The size of the library makes it necessary to introduce smarter systems as humans would not be able to cope with the number of books across the different branches.

The five examples also show typical use cases for a city. It is also interesting to note that the risk related to the services is rather low. The chatbots can provide wrong or useless answers but beyond that there are no risks involved. The library-related systems can lead to lower user satisfaction if books are not available or out of stock. However, it is hard to imagine that a recommendation engine for a public library can do serious harm.

3.6 Use of AI in the labor market

The labor market is a natural environment for AI. The labor market is a fuzzy environment, and it is not entirely clear which skills are relevant and important for which occupations.

For example, Deming (2017) has shown how social skills are increasingly important as jobs requiring high levels of social interactions have become more important. In the study, he found that a winning combination is math as well as social skills. Heckman and Kautz (2012) summarize personality traits, goals, motivations, and preferences as soft skills. Digital skills are another category often discussed. Van Laar et al. (2017) see information digital skills, communication digital skills, collaboration digital skills, critical-thinking digital skills, creative digital skills, and problem-solving digital skills.

In general, skills are not clearly defined. For example, European Skills, Competences, and Occupations (ESCO) defines a "skills and competences" pillar which includes knowledge, skills, and competences. Some examples are listed in the table below.

The use of multiple labels for thousands of skills is a perfect use case for the natural language-processing tools and the subset of semantic similarity (Zad et al. 2021). These tools measure the semantic similarity between two texts which can be single words or longer texts.

The following figure shows how pretrained neural networks such as the Universal Sentence Encoder can be used to show the similarity between different skills. In principle, the Universal Sentence Encoder calculates vectors in 512 dimensions for the text. These vectors can then be used to assess the similarity between different texts. The figure uses different colors to visualize the semantic similarity. The

TABLE 3.5 Examples of skills and their different labels

Reuse Level	Preferred Label	Alternative Labels	Description
Sector-specific	Operate wrecking ball	• Demolish structure with wrecking ball • Operating wrecking ball • Wrecking ball control • Wrecking ball operation • Operation of wrecking ball • Control wrecking ball • Demolition with wrecking ball	Use a wrecking ball to demolish a structure or parts of it. Hoist the wrecking ball into the air with a crane. Drop the ball or swing it in a controlled manner to hit the structure. Prevent misses as the weight and momentum of the ball may destabilize the crane.
Transversal	Write Hungarian	• Writing Hungarian • Correspond in written Hungarian • Show competency in written Hungarian	Compose written texts in Hungarian.
Occupation specific	Clean beer pipes	• Ensure beer pipes are washed clean • Clean pipes of beer • Wash beer tubes	Disinfect beer pipes on regular basis according to guidelines to ensure the beer is tasty and hygienic.
Cross-sector	Interpret religious texts	• Explain religious texts • Explain religious teachings • Clarify religious teachings • Clarify religious texts • Decipher religious teachings • Translate religious texts • Translate religious teachings • Decipher religious texts	Interpret the contents and messages of religious texts in order to develop spiritually and help others in their spiritual development, to apply the appropriate passages and messages during services and ceremonies, or for theological learning.

Source: ESCO (2022).

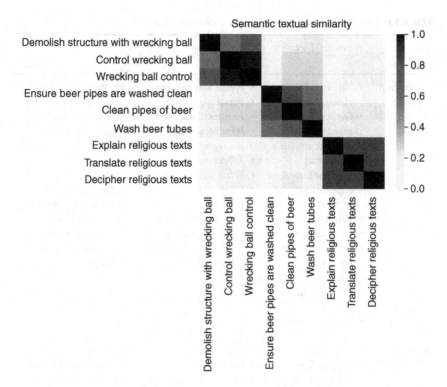

FIGURE 3.4 Semantic similarity of different labels for skills

Source: Own illustration based on Universal Sentence Encoder from TensorFlow (2022)

different clusters have been clearly identified, and such results can be used to clearly identify skills even if applicants.[4]

The next step is to identify an occupation which fits with the personal skill set. Occupations are those activities where people spend most of their time pursuing a professional career. There are different approaches to defining occupations. The following table shows some examples of different occupations together with alternative labels and longer descriptions.

The following figure shows how semantic similarity tools classify similar occupations. The tool classified "scooter technician," "bicycle fixer," and "bike repairer" correctly. However, for "supermarket cashier," "toll booth attendant," and "checkout operative," it gave lower similarity scores.

There are many applications which evaluate the performance of employees. Brown, Burke, and Sauciuc (2021) discuss the benefits of integrating AI in performance evaluation systems. The main argument to implement these tools is the idea that AI reduces the level of bias in these evaluations. Altemeyer (2019) discusses business cases where machine learning tools were used to select the best employees in the past and automatically identify similar applicants.

TABLE 3.6 Examples of occupations and their different labels

Preferred Label	Alternative Labels		Description
Fuel station manager	• Supermarket filling station manager • Gas station manager • Fuel site manager • Retail fuel forecourt manager	• Retail fuel manager • Petrol site manager • Fuel retail manager • Retail forecourt manager • Filling station manager • Petrol station manager	Fuel station managers assume responsibility for activities and staff in a fuel station.
Cashier	• Supermarket cashier • Checkout operator • Shop cashier • Toll booth attendant • Checkout operator • Department store cashier • Hypermarket cashier	• Checkout assistant • Filling station cashier • Check out assistant • Checkout operative • Outlet center cashier • Checkout operative	Cashiers operate the cash register, receive payments from customers, issue receipts and return change due.
Bicycle mechanic	• Scooter technician • Bicycle fixer • Bike repairer • Bicycle repairer • Bicycle shop attendant • Bike shop assistant • Cycle technician • Bicycle technician • Bike mechanic • Cycle mechanic	• Bike technician • Cycle repairer • Bicycle maintenance technician • Bike shop worker • Scooter mechanic • Bicycle shop assistant • Scooter repairer • Bicycle repairman • Bicycle shop worker • Bike shop attendant	Bicycle mechanics maintain and repair a variety of bicycle models and component parts. They may perform customized alterations, according to their client's preferences.
Meter reader	• Gas meter reader • Metering data reader • Electricity meter reader • Water meter reader • Smart meter reader	• Metering data analyst • Billing information analyst • Utility meter reader • Billing information reader • Smart meter data reader	Meter readers visit residential and business or industrial buildings and facilities in order to note down the readings of the meters which measure gas, water, electricity, and other utility uses. They forward the results to the client and to the supplier.

Source: ESCO (2022).

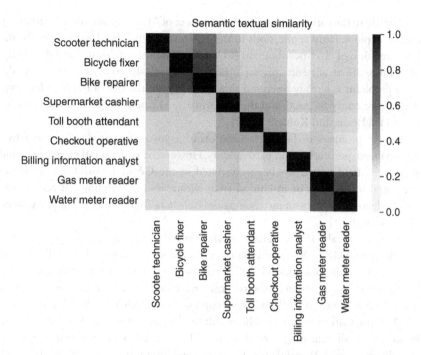

FIGURE 3.5 Semantic similarity of different labels for occupations

Source: Own illustration based on Universal Sentence Encoder from TensorFlow (2022)

None of the models discussed was somehow inclusive for the wider workforce. For example, it can be safely assumed that the algorithms punish longer phases of unemployment.

HireVue is one such example. It has already delivered 22 million job interviews. Applicants can submit videos which are then analyzed automatically.[5] The company stresses the aspects of diversity, but it is somewhat obvious that unemployed persons or persons with another first language might not perform as good as persons who are employed or the same first language as the recruiting company.

HiredScore is another example. It also stresses diversity and inclusion and promises to increase both. It is a concept for companies with many applications (more than 500,000 per year) which need to be treated consistently and somewhat automatized.

Companies who offer matching services use mostly semantic analyses. SkillLab is one concept which helps individuals to map their work experience into a set of clearly identified skills.[6] Once the model has identified a few dozen skills, it can start suggesting occupations which require these skills.

3.7   Use of AI in healthcare

Healthcare is another natural environment for the implementation of AI. Millions of data points are generated each day, and some of the tasks are repetitive. Imagine, for example, the process of analyzing X-rays in hospitals.

Already in the early stages of the development of AI, healthcare was an interesting area to explore. Early applications in the 1970s were rule-based approaches for the interpretation of electrocardiogram (ECG), the diagnoses of diseases, and the choice of appropriate treatments, among others. These rule-based systems ran into the same problems as already discussed above and explain the rise of machine learning. They were costly to build, and the performance is based on prior medical knowledge (Yu, Beam, and Kohane 2018).

AI also promises to be the foundation of a 4p-medicine which is predictive, personalized, preventive, and participatory. However, it is also a rather complex and segmented field which has been illustrated in the Covid-19 pandemic. Data are generated in hospitals or in clinical trials. Wearables measure physical activities as well as sleep patterns. Insurance companies have data about medications and general health records.

The data are also diverse. There are all forms of images such as Magnetic resonance imaging (MRI), X-ray, or ultrasound and ECG- or DNA-related information. This multimodality also makes it difficult to train AI systems (Bommasani et al. 2021).

There are two different levels to consider the impact of AI in this field. The first is on the public health level, and the second is on the individual health level.

On a population level or public health level, many have considered that AI can be used to predict flu waves or pandemics. AI was widely seen as an important tool to fight the Covid-19 pandemic. In a paper published in early 2020, Mithas et al. (2020) predicted how AI can be used to early detect disease outbreaks:

> At the population level, the availability of big datasets on population health conditions, coupled with AI algorithms, allow public health institutions to predict and prevent the onset of pandemics. Specifically, improved scan and interpret technologies detect and identify the weakest signals of a disease outbreak, thereby enabling an "early detection–early response" strategy.

However, it was not really implemented widely. Given the experiences during the Covid-19 pandemic, it seems unlikely that big data will help to predict future waves and outbreaks.

On an individual level, healthcare is a sector plagued by "Baumol's cost disease" (Baumol and Bowen 1968). Healthcare is one of the sectors which has seen little or no productivity growth. A doctor still needs the same time to diagnose a flu or finish an operation. It is exceedingly difficult to improve the productivity of healthcare. It is sensible to keep human interaction in the care for old persons or in hospitals. Anything related to emotional support and rapport will surely continue to be human focused. However, it should be added that the quality of the services increased and helped to increase the average life expectancy.

There are various tasks which can be supported with AI systems. There are also other approaches to personalizing medicine. It might be possible to personalize cancer treatments by sequencing tumors, and the use of fitness trackers might open up opportunities to detect early signs of serious health conditions.

SkinVision is a typical start-up in this area. As of early 2022, it has received $16.5 million in funding from Dutch social venture-capital fund Rubio Impact Ventures and others. The company has built a tool able to identify skin cancer by simply uploading a picture taken with a smartphone. The sensitivity of the program is 95%, and the specificity is 78%. This means that the algorithm detects 95% of (pre)malignant conditions, but it also means that 78% of all benign conditions are labeled as risky. There might be quite a few patients who are anxious about a benign lesion as outlined by Udrea et al. (2020).

So far, they have conducted 2.9 million checks for 1.8 million customers. In the process, they have detected 49,000 skin cancers. They are using a conditional adversarial network algorithm for the segmentation and support vector machine for the risk classification (Udrea et al. 2020). They have a training dataset of 130,000 images taken by 30,000 users with their smartphones. A problem remains the small set of malignant conditions. Of course, there will also remain a limited amount of malignant cases which have been confirmed in a laboratory. The total number of histopathologically validated images for skin cancer was only a few hundred. It is a small dataset to train the data.

There are also other criticisms around the methodology of the dataset creation (Deeks, Dinnes, and Williams 2020). In addition, there always remains the question how individuals will react to the alerts of the app. In other contexts, it was often found that these apps rarely work for persons with darker skins.

Freeman et al. (2021) analyze the accuracy of AI systems for image analysis in breast cancer screening. They find that 34 of 36 AI systems were less accurate than a single radiologist. None of the AI systems were more accurate than the consensus of two or more radiologists. This is still a surprising finding.

Briganti and Le Moine (2020) also point out that the clinical validation of tools and concepts will be a major challenge in the coming years. There are many open questions regarding the validation of algorithms where the data sources might be different. They also add that only a few studies compare the performance of AI systems and clinicians using the datasets.

A project in Scotland aims to use AI tools to identify the life patterns of elderly people living alone at home. When the person is not putting the kettle on, or is having a much longer shower than expected, the system will alert a contact person.[7]

There are already a range of companies developing these concepts which is often summarized as digital gerontechnology.

Rubeis (2020) adds examples of AI systems and lists various applications. Wearables or floor sensors might detect falls. Sensors might detect unusual sleep patterns or an unusual use of gas or water for dementia patients.

However, it is also important to consider ethical considerations. Rubeis (2020) introduces 4d which are depersonalization, discrimination, dehumanization, and disciplining. There are many aspects where technology can lead to unintended consequences. For example, most empirical studies are conducted on majority groups. This might lead to recommendations which are not beneficial for minorities.

3.8 Use of AI in education

Education is another sector plagued by Baumol's cost disease. Education has changed little over the centuries with teachers still standing in front of a classroom. Of course, tablets and other digital tools have been introduced, but changes are happening at a slow pace.

Education is also another natural environment for AI tools. The output is relatively clear (e.g., good test scores), but every student has his or her own learning pace and path. In addition, the abundance of data (e.g., 3 million questions answered each week in the case of one UK-based provider) is an enabler for developing new tools.

The London-based company Century – described as "Netflix for education" – is able to offer personalized learning using the data it collects.[8] Different AI-based algorithms are used to predict the best learning journeys for the students.

AI can contribute at four different levels (Kučak, Juričić, and Đambić 2018). It can be used to grade students. It makes sense when teaching takes place online, but it also enables teachers to spend more time with their students. AI systems can also be implemented to improve student retention. These systems can also be used to identify students which are at risk of leaving their school or university. AI systems have also been shown to be able to predict student performance. Future expected student performance can be used to match students or suggest ways to improve their performance. Finally, AI systems can also be used to test students.

uPlanner is a Chile-based company which has received $5 million in funding from Acumen LatAm Impact Ventures and other venture-capital funds. One of their services is the prediction of student performance.

They illustrate their work with an example of a student (uPlanner 2016):

1. *He got accepted in Mechanical Engineering at one of the best universities of the world, located at a massive campus in central Mexico, with a population of over 40,000 students.*
2. *On his application, he stated that Mechanics was his second choice, after he was rejected from Computer Engineering at the same institution.*
3. *He began getting excellent grades and won a half tuition scholarship. Furthermore, his library records show he spent a substantial amount of time at the library browsing through selected books.*

However, from the second year of school, something happened:

1. *His time and attendance records dropped: he began skipping lectures on the eve of weekends.*
2. *His records showed that he began living at a student residence, as his hometown was over 700 km away from campus.*
3. *His financial form provided evidence that his parents had used a loan to pay for education, but that over previous months these payments were delayed. Pedro may be at risk of dropping out due to financial and geographical reasons.*

This is a typical example for a case which is beyond human recognition capabilities. Each student has a different profile, and it might be impossible to create rules and early identify students at risk of leaving their studies.

As of 2020, they are serving 200 campuses with 2.5 million students. In total, 80% are coming from low-income and underserved backgrounds (ImpactAlpha 2021).

3.9 Use of AI to improve the lives of persons with disabilities

Persons with disabilities often face barriers in society. It starts with accessibility in the public transport system, access to judicial systems, inclusive education, or access to the labor market.

Much has happened over the last few decades. One of the key developments was the UN Convention on the Rights of Persons with Disabilities which was adopted in 2006 (United Nations Department of Economic and Social Affairs Disability 2022).

However, there is still much to do when it comes to persons with disabilities. disabilities. Consider the complexity of transcribing speech to text. It is almost impossible to come up with rules to transcribe conversations or speeches, but neural networks inspired by the human brain are good tools to achieve these outcomes. Speech-to-text tools are widely spread and have significant benefits for the clients.

French-based AVA is one of the companies which has developed a tool that translates speech to text specifically targeting deaf individuals.[9] AVA has so far raised $8 million in venture-capital funding and supports more than 150,000 clients a day.

It positions its service as "live captioning" and aims to target the 450 million deaf and hard-of-hearing people globally. It listens to conversations and instantly captures them on a screen for an instantaneous understanding of the conversation.

Individuals who have difficulties being understood can train their own individual neural network with Israeli-based Voiceitt.[10] This service is quite impressive, helping people who suffer from speech impairment caused by strokes, Amyotrophic lateral sclerosis Amyotrophic lateral sclerosis (ALS), or Parkinson's disease, among others, to be understood.

It understands its services as an app for people with nonstandard speech. Not being understood is a major hurdle for people with disabilities. An individual can train phrases with the app, and the AI system can understand any phrase after 30 repetitions.

There are many persons who have a form of communication disorder. These disorders are related to Parkinson disease, brain tumor, or cerebral palsy, among others. This means that they cannot be easily understood and need some form of speech-generating device (Murero et al. 2020). It has a high social value. The speaker can train the system to understand phrases he wants to use.

3.10 Use of AI in agriculture and the fight against climate change

The data structure in agricultural settings is interesting for AI-based applications. There is only one result, but a large variance for the input variables. Farmers usually want to maximize the crop yield, while they need to consider sunshine days, rainfall, humidity, or earth quality.

There are a few problems when it comes to the implementation of AI in agriculture (OECD 2019). Many of the emerging concepts require extensive sensors and good infrastructure. This is often not available. In addition, farmers have different mindsets than entrepreneurs and might not necessarily embrace modern equipment which enable high-precision farming. Moreover, these equipment and machinery often require large investments.

Many companies are already working in this space. Israeli-based Prospera monitors 4,700 agricultural fields and processes 50 million data points per day.[11] Cape Town's Aerobotics is using satellite images and drone flights to monitor crops, collecting data to identify patterns and potential improvements for the management of fields. Crop One in California is pioneering vertical farming. Vertical farms can easily be equipped with sensors to generate data that can then be used to improve the yield.

Tackling and understanding the effects of climate change with machine learning is another topic as discussed by Rolnick et al. (2019). Imagine that you want to count how many animals of a certain species are living in an area. Usually, this involves species counting, which is very labor intensive. However, image recognition and classification is a well-established AI tool that can be implemented to identify even individual animals.

A closely related topic is food security. Decuyper et al. (2014) show that there is a relatively high correlation between mobile-phone data and expenditure on food or vegetable consumption. The data are relatively unstructured but can be used to predict food shortages or provide a multidimensional poverty index.

Other examples include Cervest which provides risk data related to climate change for each building or stretch of land. It is a service for investors or companies that want to identify the risks associated with certain climate hazards for tangible assets. The company is also using AI tools to generate signals and additional insights from the petabytes of climate data they are working with.[12]

Munich-based OroraTech is detecting wildfires using satellite data. They are launching their own complementary satellites which help them to increase the coverage of the area. Interestingly, they run neural networks on board of the satellites to detect trails of smoke. This is still in the research and developing stage but could potentially be very effective.[13]

The Swedish start-up Ignitia has recently raised $4.2 million for a tropical weather forecasting platform. It is expected to have over 84% reliability, and it

TABLE 3.7 Examples of AI-based business models in agriculture

Category	Company	Description
Agricultural robotics	Abundant Robotics	Developed an apple-vacuum robot that uses computer vision to detect and pick apples with the same accuracy and care as a human. The company claims that the work of one robot is equivalent to that of ten people.
	Blue River Technology	Developed a robot known as See & Spray to monitor plants and soils and spray herbicide on weeds in lettuce and cotton fields. Precision spraying can help prevent resistance to herbicide and decrease the volume of chemicals used by 80%. John Deere acquired this company in September 2017 at USD 305 million.
	Harvest CROO Robotics	Developed a robot to help pick and pack strawberries. It can harvest 3.2 hectares a day and replace 30 human workers, helping to address labor shortage in key farming regions and prevent associated revenue losses.
Crop and soil monitoring	PEAT	Developed a deep-learning application to identify potential soil defects and nutrient deficiencies. It diagnoses plant health based on images taken by farmers.
	Resson	Developed image recognition algorithms that can accurately detect and classify plant pests and diseases. Resson has partnered with McCain Foods to help minimize losses in the potato production supply chain.
	SkySquirrel Technologies	Developed a system to analyze vineyard health based on images. Users upload images by drones to the company's cloud system that diagnoses grapevine leaves' condition. The company claims its technology can scan 20 hectares in 24 minutes and provide data analysis with 95% accuracy.
Predictive analytics	aWhere	Developed machine learning algorithms based on satellite data to predict weather conditions and provide customized advice to farmers, crop consultants, and researchers. It also provides users with access to over a billion points of agronomic data daily.
	FarmShots	Developed a system to analyze agricultural data derived from satellite and drone images. The system can detect diseases, pests, and poor plant nutrition on farms and inform users precisely where their fields need fertilizer, reducing the amount used by nearly 40%.

Source: OECD (2019) based on company descriptions.

sends its forecast via SMS to West African farmers.[14] They describe their AI-based approach as:

> Recently, Ignitia's R&D team has started developing a machine learning model to tackle this problem of nowcasting thunderstorms over a period of three hours (to begin with). Based on almost a decade of down-to-the-second timing and position of individual thunderstorms in the West Africa region, patterns are emerging that machine learning techniques are picking up and that complements our probabilistic ensemble forecasting system. Our goal is to create a model that will be able to learn/mirror the dynamics of the storm for a number of time steps into the future.

Notes

1 For more information, see www.kaggle.com/. There is also a Google search function for datasets identifying public datasets. For more information, see https://datasetsearch.research.google.com/
2 For more information, see www.saildrone.com/solutions/ocean-data
3 See https://ai.hel.fi/en/ai-register/
4 Another process is the identification of skills acquired over a lifetime and bring them into a CV form. For example, Rezi uses GPT-3 to write CVs. For more information, see www.rezi.ai/
5 For more information, see www.hirevue.com/
6 For more information, see https://skilllab.io/en-us
7 This example gives an impression of the continuous amount of data that have to be analyzed. For more information, see www.nesta.org.uk/feature/ai-good-meet-grantees/blackwood-homes-and-care/
8 For more information, see www.century.tech/ and www.century.tech/news/how-does-centurys-ai-work/
9 www.ava.me/
10 www.voiceitt.com/why-voiceitt.html or www.youtube.com/watch?v=CoY3G7O-M1s
11 https://home.prospera.ag/about, www.aerobotics.com/, and https://cropone.ag/technology
12 For more information, see https://cervest.earth/
13 For more information, see https://ororatech.com/
14 For more information, see www.ignitia.se/

4
AI AND IMPACT FINANCE

4.1 Introduction

Finance is a functional science as its sole purpose should be to support societal goals (Shiller 2013), although a significant number of financial activities are of a speculative nature. This chapter covers the role of artificial intelligence (AI) to create social value through the financial sector.

The use of statistical models is not new for the financial sector. There is a complete industry built around quantitative investment strategies. One of the leading hedge funds in this field has built its track record on machine learning. Renaissance Capital is led by a former mathematician who bet on relationships that have been identified by algorithms (Zuckerman 2019). For example, an increase of a certain currency might reduce the price of a certain commodity. It is not clear which factors can explain this relationship, but it is the basis of a profitable trading strategy.

AI is thus useful for analyzing large amounts of data to find patterns. These patterns can be investment returns, fraud patterns, or loan decisions. Credit scoring and loan decisions are relatively structured problems. It is mainly concerned with the prediction if a certain loan will be repaid or not. Large financial institutions are deploying AI across their operations. At the client-facing front office, they are already relying on robo advisors or chatbots.

AI is also used for the private and public equity markets. In the public equity markets, it is more about general factors such as valuation levels and multiples. Investors do not need to consider exit strategies as shares are usually liquid. In the private equity markets, there are many different value drivers. Investors consider leverage ratios, exit opportunities, market timing, and negotiations skills, among others.

DOI: 10.4324/9781003218913-4

In principle, there are three options to create impact with finance:

1. Underserved segments of the population receive access to finance
2. Capital is provided to investments promising higher impact
3. Impact enterprises receive access to finance

The dominant view has long been influenced by Friedman (1970). He argued that companies should purely consider the business objectives and leave philanthropic funding to their shareholders. Milton Friedman famously wrote that the only social responsibility of business is to maximize profits. This led to structures in which the profit motive was dominant, and stakeholders were seen as less relevant as shareholders.

This has begun to change. Hart and Zingales (2017) argue in an influential article that companies should consider the pro-social preferences of their shareholders. These considerations are still at the core of larger discussions.

In a recent example, a stakeholder-oriented company was taken over by a tobacco company purely based on financial criteria when Philip Morris International (PMI) acquired Vectura. Vectura is a company which produces inhalers combating respiratory diseases and it always stressed the value it generates for stakeholders including employees, suppliers, and patients. However, the board accepted the acquisition offer from the tobacco company instead of a private equity group (*The Economist* 2021). An independent ownership structure might be more attractive for employees and patients but ultimately equity owners preferred a slightly higher offer neglecting the interests of the other stakeholders.

Asset owners are those at the core of the discussions. They provide the capital for investment activities, but they also decide which asset manager or investment manager should take decisions on their behalf and can even structure the compensation accordingly.

Impact-linked pricing can take place across the investment value chain (Boggild 2021). Asset owners can link the compensation of the investment managers to the delivery of intended outcomes. Investment managers can link the payments of the business to the delivery of intended consequences. The same can happen between the company and the end customer.

It is possible to create impact across different asset classes. These asset classes include cash, bonds, private equity, or real estate, among others.

Cash is an asset class where it is relatively difficult to create impact. Some companies have decided to leave their cash with banks and financial institutions targeting low-income communities. For example, Netflix has decided to move $100 million or 2% of their cash reserves to Black banks and other Black-led financial institutions (Vardi 2020). This gives the banks additional capital to invest in their communities.

The role of public equities involves the question which companies to invest in. For example, it is possible to invest in bonds as well as equity of public companies. Private equity is the financing form with the most structuring flexibility.

There are many opportunities when it comes to real estate. Examples are social housing or generational housing projects.

It should also be added that many individuals and foundations also provide grants to organizations they want to support.

In general, it is a fast evolving space. In the last years, we have seen financing mechanisms and new investment styles focused on social, environmental, or governance-related areas. There are also new forms of financing mechanisms which structure financing in new forms such as revenue share agreements.

4.2 Historical overview with a focus on credit scoring

Banking used to be a relationship business. Bank officers knew their clients and knew their creditworthiness. There were no extensive documents or datasets to assess the likelihood of repayments. Loan decisions were based on personal relationships and gut feelings often referred to as 3Cs, 4Cs, or even 5Cs (Thomas 2000):

- The character of the person – do you know the person or their family?
- The capital – how much is being asked for?
- The collateral – what is the applicant willing to put up from their own resources?
- The capacity – what is their repaying ability. How much free income do they have?
- The condition – what are the conditions in the market?

Formal credit scoring was first introduced in the 1960s and was first used for credit cards. Organizations soon realized that automatic lending decisions lead to dramatically lower default rates. The US Equal Credit Opportunity Act even outlawed discrimination in credit decision unless they can be statistically justified. The ideas pioneered in the area of credit cards soon migrated into other products such as personal and business loans (Thomas 2000).

In the 1980s, logistic regression and linear programming were introduced in optimizing the process of providing loans (Thomas 2000). Logistic regressions remain a standard tool for credit scoring and evaluating the creditworthiness of borrowers (Dastile, Celik, and Potsane 2020).

Logistic regression models work well as financial institutions need to make transparent credit decisions, and transparency and accountability are part of the regulation requirements.

In the last years, machine learning algorithms have been more widely used. There are many claiming that a few data points are sufficient to assess the personality or even the creditworthiness of individuals.

Finance is a topic which is especially relevant for AI. Financial institutions have very large datasets which they need to analyze. Each transaction is a data point they can use. There is only one variable they need to consider. For banks, it is the risk of default and non-repayment. For quantitative investors, it is the potential return of an investment.

Imagine the available data points for a single individual. There are hundreds of account transactions which give a good overview of the profile. It involves the counterparts, salaries, or revenues for a company.

For a company, there are even more data points. Companies need to submit financial reports, but there are also good data points on the regularity of income streams, the cost structures, and the on-time payment of bills.

It would not be very efficient for individual loan officers to analyze the different income streams. In addition, there are profit opportunities when it comes to analyzing large amounts of data.

AI can help to reduce the costs to check different kinds of documents and contracts. Some of the early fintechs such as PayPal pioneered the identification of fraudulent payments. AI systems are very suited for identifying patterns in big data.

DemystData is a New York-based data company which has raised $56 million so far. Accion Venture Lab which is connected to the nonprofit organization of the same name was one of the earlier investors and led the Series A investment round.[1] At the beginning, it was meant to improve the underserved communities and the socioeconomic base of the pyramid.

DemystData is now offering an ecosystem to financial institutions which can pull data from multiple sources to inform their decision-making processes. Among the 588 data sources are registries of business bankruptcies, fraud indicators, corporate registrations, or all other forms of information of interest for financial institutions.

Data and information have been a scarce resource for decades. The commodity business is a good example of how data became widely available. Until the 1980s, prices of a commodity were not easily available. Blas and Farchy (2021) describe how information was once the secret of some trading houses where suppliers in Zambia, Peru, or Mongolia had no access to current information of prices and were often using the prices of last week. This began to change in the 1980s. Today, even farmers have access to market data with their phones via SMS. The same applies to information about shortages, strikes, or similar developments. It is now easily available via the internet and not anymore the secret of international trading houses.

4.3 Finance for underserved segments of the population

Large segments of the population in low- and middle-income countries do not have access to banking services. They are often called "unbanked." This is a problem as shown in a large body of academic literature which analyzes the relationship between economic growth and financial institutions.

Following Sarma (2008), financial inclusion can be defined "as a process that ensures the ease of access, availability and usage of the formal financial system for all members of an economy." If it is defined via exclusion, it is possible to differentiate between voluntary and involuntary exclusion (Park and Mercado 2018). Some might refuse to use financial services due to religious reasons or a lack of need. More problematic is the involuntary exclusion. This happens because of high risks associated with the target groups or market failures.

Traditionally, there was a focus on microcredit. Over time, it was referred to as microfinance as it also included other services such as savings, investments, and insurances (Mhlanga 2020).

There have been many initiatives to increase access to finance. Among the first initiatives were those implemented with mobile payment system M-PESA.[2] It was and still is an innovative payment system based on text messages.

Mhlanga (2020) describes the trade-off of concepts such as Grameen as a traditional microfinance institution and fintechs. The traditional microfinance institutions have a presence in the field and close interactions with their target groups. Fintechs put their emphasis on digital services and do not require offices close to their customers.

Microfinance in general has to find sustainable business models with relatively little margins. Clients often have capital needs of $500 or less. In addition, it is often the first loan, and they need additional support to develop their business. This limits the amount which can be charged for overhead expenses.

A lack of credit history leads to higher risks for the financial institutions, but at the same the lack of access to finance is a problem for large parts of the population in emerging countries (e.g., Geremewe 2019; Sharma et al. 2021).

The first area where AI systems are relevant is in the provision of loans to persons outside of the formal financial system. In principle, it is the following situation. A financial institution has information about the age, gender, income, employment or income, transaction record, and the repayment rate of persons with a similar profile.

A static statistical model would predict the rate of repayment given a certain set of indicators such as gender, age, income, and educational levels. AI systems can expand the existing data and integrate every data source to predict the repayment rate.

AI systems can also contribute to lower the costs of loan provision. Some fintech can provide loans with automated systems at costs of a few cents. AI systems have also been shown to be able to forecast the credit risk for agricultural small- and medium-sized enterprises (SMEs)' investments (Belhadi et al. 2021).

TABLE 4.1 Typical credit-related information on clients

Person	Age	Income	...	Repayment
1	48	2,000	...	Yes
2	27	3,190	...	Yes
3	58	980	...	Yes
...		...	...	No
n	33	1,740	...	Yes

Source: Own illustration.

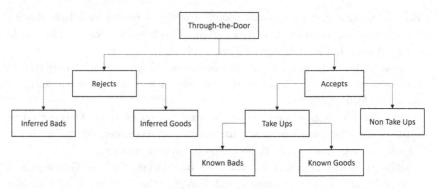

FIGURE 4.1 Different outcomes of credit-related decisions

Source: Own illustration based on Dastile, Celik, and Potsane (2020)

Credit scoring is a straightforward problem. The models try to predict which individuals or companies are likely to repay their loan. It is thus a binary classification problem. It is also a supervised learning problem as the model can be trained on a dataset with clear labels.

The underlying economic theory is that there is an information asymmetry between the financial institution and the borrower. It means that one party knows less than the other party which is usually the case in credit decisions.

This means that a financial institution needs to have access to as much information as possible. A high degree of information asymmetry can lead to market failures as it prevents the efficient allocation of capital to enterprises and individuals.

In principle, lenders need to rely on the willingness of borrowers to repay the loan. Moral hazard is the phenomenon that borrowers might take the decision not to repay the loan.

Dastile, Celik, and Potsane (2020) list as commonly used statistical techniques linear discriminant analysis (LDA), logistic regression (LR), and Naïve Bayes (NB), and the machine learning include k-nearest neighbor (k-NN), decision trees (DTs), support vector machines (SVMs), artificial neural networks (ANNs), random forests (RFs), boosting, extreme gradient boost (XGBoost), bagging, restricted Boltzmann machines (RBMs), deep multilayer perceptron (DMLP), convolutional neural networks (CNNs), and deep belief neural networks (DBNs). The list is a reminder showing the range of different models which can be used for credit scoring.

Dastile, Celik, and Potsane (2020) report that databases usually contain much more data on good borrowers than on defaulting borrowers. A European sample contains almost 187,000 borrowers, whereas 180,000 were classified as good borrowers, while only 7,000 were classified as bad borrowers. This is similar to the healthcare problem discussed above and impacts the possibilities to predict bad borrowers.

Nowadays, credit officers and credit modelers can access a range of alternative data. For example, some funds want to access online sales data from clients to assess

TABLE 4.2 Use of digital footprints for credit-related decisions

Company	Main Region	Digital Footprint Usage
Klarna	Europe	Uses time-of-the-day in its scoring model, states that it collects e-mail host, device type, browser settings, operating system, and screen resolution to evaluate which payment methods to make available
Admiral Insurance Group	UK	Drivers applying with a "Hotmail" e-mail address are charged higher insurance fees, as the company finds that some e-mail domain names are associated with more accidents than others
Sesame Credit	China	Sesame Credit gives users a score based on five dimensions of information: personal information, payment ability, credit history, social networks, and online behaviors
LenddoEFL	Emerging markets	Uses variables such as smartphone data, form-filling analytics, text length, browser data, mouse data, Wi-Fi networks used, or even phone battery life
ZestFinance	United States	Applies machine learning and "Google-like math to credit decisions" on thousands of potential credit variables including proper spelling and capitalization in online application forms, time of day making online purchases
Branch International	Africa	Uses mobile phone data, including grammar and punctuation in text messaging, time of day of calls to evaluate potential borrowers
Cignifi	Emerging markets	Partnering with leading global Telco brands, including Telefónica, AT&T, Globe Telecom, and Cignifi, uses mobile phone data, call duration, time calls are made, numbers frequently called, who initiates calls, or the frequency of adding airtime credit on prepaid phones
KrediTech	Emerging markets	Uses AI and machine learning, processing up to 20,000 data points per application. Simple variables, such as device data and operating systems, are used. Also, different behavioral analytics (movement and duration on the Web page) or even the font installed on the computer, the time spent filling out the online application, or whether the customer copy and pastes input data play a role in the scoring model

Source: Based on Berg et al. (2020).

if they are eligible for loans. Some loan providers are checking the social media profiles.

There are endless consumer data points. There is also enough skepticism toward these models as they impact privacy concerns and reinforce structural injustices. For example, if one person has poor friends, it would be unfair to reduce his chances to receive a loan.

Some companies are already trying to calculate the creditworthiness of businesses or individuals using alternative data points. Berg et al. (2020) show how consumers using Apple devices, paid e-mail hosts, or having their name in the e-mail address have lower default rates. The company's model is based on these criteria, and consumers not using Apple devices have a disadvantage.

The table shows some examples of digital footprint usages. All of them seem problematic. For example, applicants who are not able to spell properly are sanctioned. This is especially relevant for dyslexics and for those with another mother language. It is also possible to detect influential or important clients by analyzing the call patterns. Calls from persons with a higher status are more likely to be accepted or called back sooner in case the call was missed.

Dastile, Celik, and Potsane (2020) name two major issues with the use of machine learning tools in credit scoring which sound familiar to the issues faced in other areas. The first issue is that machine learning models are incapable of explaining their predictions. The second issue is related to the imbalances in the datasets.

The main problem is that datasets can be biased, and there are a number of reasons for this. If the underlying data are biased, it will also impact the final credit score.

Hassani (2021) conducted an interesting experiment. The approach is to predict the gender and the ethnicity based on the data used for credit scoring. The author was able to predict the gender and the ethnicity for both datasets. For example, the first dataset contained information about the income of the applicants, credit rating, credit limit, ethnicity, gender, and level of education. Using these data, the researcher was able to derive the ethnicity of the applicant. The same was true for a gender dataset. While the datasets were rather small, it points toward the biases in the existing datasets.

4.4 Impact fintechs

There are already a few impact-oriented fintechs which use AI in the processes of providing loans to individuals.

Destácame is an alternative credit scoring platform based in Chile. The service was launched in 2015. Accion Venture Lab invested in 2017.[3] The problem in many countries across Latin America is a lack of formal credit bureaus. The platform has created an algorithm which builds an alternative credit score taking into account other sources of data. These are mostly utility payment transactions which are supposed to be a proxy for payment behaviors.

The platform is trying to predict which applicants will default on the loans and which might be good borrowers. Using machine learning models led to significant improvements over the previously deployed models used at the platform. Destácame is also selling the scores to financial institutions which can use these scores to inform their loan decisions. However, the sale is subject to the approval of the clients.

Platform work will continue to increase its relevance over the coming years. One of the main challenges is to improve the social security and offers for these platform workers (Spiess-Knafl 2018).

Indian KarmaLife is a platform which uses AI to offer services.[4] KarmaLife is offering its services to Indian platform workers who do not have the same access to traditional banking services as other employees. This can be explained with a lack of historical data and limited understanding of the payment patterns. The company is partnering with crowd-working platforms to have access to the history of the work on the platforms. The user is paying a subscription fee for these services. The company is offering a dynamic credit line which is linked to the income from the user.

The user can unlock more benefits over time. Once the company has a longer track record, they can also increase the credit line. The company is offering small loans which are less than the monthly income. The main data are the work history on the platforms related to mobility, food, or flexi-staffing, among others.

Across Africa, only a small percentage of the population have a credit score and less than 20% have loans. That means that there are many opportunities for financial institutions as well as a large demand from the unbanked segments from the population.

Indicina is based in Nigeria and has so far raised more than $4 million in venture capital funding.[5] They are offering a credit infrastructure based on AI tools. They are calling it "Lending as a service" and offer to provide the complete digital process.

From an AI perspective, their credit modeling is the most interesting part. They are building the model on different expense categories. The expense categories include bills, religious giving, club and bars, gambling, utilities and internet, cable TV, airtime, and bank charges as shown in the table below. It is somewhat troubling that it is unclear if religious giving reduces or increases the probability of receiving credit. In general, this is the downside of big data and AI-based credit modeling.

It is rather unknown, but India is the third largest producer of fish in the world. A large percentage is produced in the aquaculture sector. It is a risky sector as diseases, algae blooms, typhoons, and earthquakes all pose dangers to the ponds. In addition, the cooperatives and associations all need access to finance to expand their activities (Singh 2015).

Aquaconnect is an Indian start-up founded in 2017.[6] It has raised $9 million until early 2022. It has different business lines which all address the issues above. It offers farmers suggestions on how they can improve their productivity. Farmers can upload pictures, and the app will suggest ways to improve water quality, aquatic health, or feeding. This is based on an AI system and reduces the operational risk of the business.

It also offers an interesting link to formal finance. The company is using the existing data and matches it with satellite data to provide information to insurers and financial institutions. This is an interesting example of the financialization of AI-based companies.

TABLE 4.3 Range of variables used for credit modeling

Income Analysis	Cash Flow Analysis	Spend Analysis	Behavioral analysis	Transaction Pattern Analysis
Average salary	Total credit turnover	Average recurring expenses	Inflow to outflow rate	Last date of credit
Expected salary day	Total debit turnover	Monthly value of outbound transfers	Loan amount	Last date of credit
Salary frequency	Average balance	Expense categories	Loan repayments	Highest month and week of credit
Median income	Net average monthly earnings	ATM withdrawals	Loan to inflow rate	Highest month and week of debit
Latest salary date	Account activity	Internet purchases	Loan repayment to inflow rate	Month and week with zero balance in account
Number of salary payments	Duration in statement	Spend on point of sales	Top transfer recipient account	Recurring expenses
Number of other income payments	The period in statement	USSD transactions	Top incoming transfer account	Transaction categories
Confidence intervals on salary detection	First and last days of bank statement	International transactions	Gambling rate	Most frequent balance range
	Balance at statement end	Total expenses	Account sweep	Most frequent transaction range

Source: Indicina (2022).

4.5 Provision of capital to investments promising higher impact

One of the larger questions in this research field is the relationship between financial returns and social impact. The results depend on the time frame, the methodology, and the sample. Some find that companies with a strong corporate social responsibility (CSR) profile outperform their peers (e.g., Friede, Busch, and Bassen 2015; Huang 2021), while others find the opposite (e.g., Saygili, Arslan, and Birkan 2021). However, there are also many studies which have found no significant relationships (e.g., Landi and Sciarelli 2018).

At the core, it is about the relationship between the corporate social performance and the corporate financial performance. Some argue that a good corporate social performance leads to a good corporate financial performance which leads to a more valuable company. This could be the case if a company is providing support to vulnerable groups or is active for minority rights and clients value this corporate approach.

Others argue that only those companies with a good corporate financial performance are able to exhibit good corporate social performance as it is costly to be a good corporate citizen. This good corporate social performance enhances its corporate reputation which is again good for its financial performance. Another group argues that it is an interdependent relationship and not easily distinguishable.

Green companies have been found to have lower costs of capital than those without a green profile. The lower cost of capital can be explained through lower environmental liability risk as well as higher demand from investors (El Ghoul et al. 2018). As an investor, it is thus relevant to identify those companies which have lower liability risks.

Environmental, social, and corporate governance (ESG) investing is a new field which takes the performance of companies related to these three areas into account. It involves an analysis of nonfinancial data and is becoming a mainstream approach to investing as these factors are increasingly seen as growth and profitability driver and also reduce the investment risks. There are less unknown risks when the company has clean supply chains, low levels of pollution and energy consumption, and functioning governance mechanisms.

Public equity markets are an interesting environment as there is an abundance of data to analyze. All financial information is public and easily available. In addition, all financial information is consistent and externally verified.

Publicly listed companies also publish additional information and are usually covered extensively in newspapers and other news media sources. The abundance of data and the relatively clear results make it an interesting environment for AI.

There are two main approaches to scoring and analyzing companies for their ESG scores.

The traditional analyst-driven ESG research approach starts with developing a methodology to rate companies. It would then collect, process, and analyze the data to generate a rating.

The AI-driven ESG research takes a different approach. It still needs to start with a methodology and algorithms, but the algorithm is learning on its own how to generate ratings (Hughes, Urban, and Wójcik 2021).

The first step is the collection of data. There are already some news aggregators such as Aylien which give access to more than 80,000 news media sources. The costs for this access depend on the level of services but are usually in the range of $10,000–$100,000.

All AI-based providers of ESG data work comparably. They collect and aggregate content from web news, traditional media, or alternative data sources. On a document level, the text needs to be translated and categorized. Tools can assess the sentiment of the article and extract relevant features. These data points are then aggregated on a collective level.

The result from the analysis needs to be transformed into signals and insights. The main results are scores reflecting public perceptions and public sentiments toward the company segregated across different dimensions. Researchers have found relationships between ESG scores and future market developments and have illustrated ways how they can be implemented to improve the investment decisions (e.g., De Franco et al. 2020; Serafeim 2020; Cheema-Fox et al. 2021).

A major difficulty is to map the insights to certain criteria. Some investors want to invest with a focus on biodiversity, democracy, anti-corruption, low-carbon emissions, fair salaries, clean supply chain, or good education to name among a few. AI-based companies need to structure the output and signals in such a way that investors can use the insights to select suitable companies.

There are a few data providers which aim to assess the ESG scores using machine learning approaches.

Although the methodologies should be publicly available, they mostly remain a black box. The data providers in this space are Arabesque, TruValue Labs, or Clarity AI.

TruValue Labs is the largest provider among them. The company was founded in 2013 and was acquired by FactSet in 2020. They analyze 75,000 data sources and cover more than 8,000 companies. More than half of the companies are based in North America.

They are using natural language processing tools to analyze the data sources in 13 languages. The text comes from news media, trade journals, or industry reports. It would be impossible to cover this amount of data manually.

The company is mapping the signals against the Sustainable Development Goals (SDGs) as well as the Sustainability Accounting Standard Board (SASB).

Clarity AI is another company in this space. At the end of 2021, they have finished a funding round of $50 million led by SoftBank Vision Fund. They are analyzing more than 30,000 companies and 135,000 funds.

Arabesque is based in Frankfurt and offers similar services as Clarity AI and TruValue Labs. So far, they have raised $20 million to develop their products.

The existing AI-based companies as well as the analyst-based companies have faced a series of critiques in the past.

Most of the ratings and scores lack ambitious targets. It is often a positive sign to have a 20% share of women in senior management positions or to have a safe working environment. Many investors do not find these targets very ambitious and would prefer to see more meaningful targets. Some targets are just in line with legal requirements and should not lead to higher ESG scores.

AI has the problem that the findings are impossible to replicate. AI-based ESG data providers are black boxes which provide no information on how they calculate their numbers. In addition, there is no information on what kind of data they are using to inform their calculations. This is troubling given that they are responsible for directing billions of capital flows toward impactful areas.

In addition, these scores have rarely been found to predict scandals. Some scores have highlighted problematic practices, but there are no cases where ESG scores predicted any major breaking scandals. It is also obvious that fraudulent behavior such as in the cases of Enron, German payment provider Wirecard, or Volkswagen is impossible to predict.

Another problem is the lack of tested standards as well as inconsistent and patchy data. Financial data are verified by auditors, but there are no comparable procedures for nonfinancial data on the environmental or social targets.

4.6 Access to finance for impact enterprises

A small investment fund usually receives more than 1,000 investment proposals per year and typically invests in less than 1% of the investment opportunities. The proportion of investments depends on the marketing activities of the fund, the investment focus, and the general market environment.

Funds are receiving rather diverse sets of materials. Some entrepreneurs share relatively detailed business plans and financials, while others only share a description of the idea and the team behind it.

Investment managers are thus trying to identify good companies and investing in those with the best outlook. This implies that it is relatively complicated to train such models given the quality and consistency of the data.

AI tools can be used to conduct a number of investment analyses and to identify general trends. Natural language processing is used to analyze patent registration, identify innovation clusters, or identify outperforming companies. This might lead to the identification of relatively unknown start-ups.

AI can also be used to score potential investments. Ross et al. (2021) develop a model which predicts the outcome of investments. The model is based on data covering intellectual property ownership from the United States Patent and Trademark Office (USPTO) as well as company and funding information from Crunchbase.

The following paragraph describes their approach in experimenting with the structure of neural network they are using to predict the outcome of the investments.

> We experimented with many configurations, tweaking the number of hidden layers, number of neurons in each layer, and regularization. The best results were obtained from a relatively simple network comprised of five hidden layers with 32 neurons in each, interspersed with alternating dropout layers with dropout rate set to 0.2. For efficiency, the rectified linear activation function (ReLU) was used for every layer with the exception of the last. Given the goal is to classify every private company into one of three classes with a specific probability, as in the exit case, this is deemed a multi-label problem and therefore the softmax activation function was selected for the last layer and the chosen loss function of choice was sparse categorical cross-entropy.
>
> Experimentation with MLP models of lesser complexity produced increased loss while more complex models showed signs of overfitting.

With this model, Ross et al. (2021) are able to predict outcomes (initial public offering [IPO], acquisition, failure) and follow-on funding with an accuracy of 80%–89%. There are a few limitations as market cycles are changing, and features which are relevant in 2015 might not be relevant in 2022. In addition, it is hard to explain the model.

Another problem is related to the exit strategies of the funds. The social finance industry is still a young industry. The vintage years of the majority of funds are in the period between 2015 and 2020. That means that there are not too many cases of exits.

In general, there are different exit strategies for different financing instruments.

For equity capital, there needs to be some kind of transaction. A secondary market is not widely developed which explains why many funds are focusing on debt capital as there is no need for transactions at the end of the investment period. Mezzanine capital is a combination of equity and debt capital. It has the advantage that there is a fixed repayment after 3–7 years and a potential upside through equity-like components.

Many large consumer goods companies have acquired impact enterprises in the past. The business case seems to be that the customer base is loyal and is also willing to pay higher prices for the products.

TOMS is a good example for this investment rationale. TOMS was founded in 2006. It pioneered the model of buying one and giving one. It was a very successful model, and revenues in 2013 reached $250 million. In 2014, Bain Capital acquired a 50% stake at an enterprise valuation of $625 million. Bain Capital was committed to continue the "one-for-one" policy.

In 2019, creditors took over the company in 2019 as the company was not able to repay a $300 million loan. Media reports mentioned that the "one-for-one" was wearing off, competitors lowered prices, and there was increased criticism. The company has gifted close to 95 million pairs of shoes to children. It also caused major disruptions in local markets.

There are also examples where investors focus on rising valuation. In the last years, companies have raised significant amounts of capital. France-based Ÿnsect which is farming insects raised $425 million funding, Dutch Mosa Meat which produces alternative meat raised $96 million, and Hong Kong-based Green Monday Holdings which also produces alternative meat has raised $70 million so far. It can be concluded that many funds invested on an investment thesis of rising valuations in this space following the success of Beyond Meat after its IPO.

In general, there are few investment theses we can observe. Some are focusing on stable and low-risk impact enterprises and finance them with loans. It is many driven by the fact that stable and low risk implies that there is not enough potential for equity investments.

Another group focuses on asset-backed impact enterprises and also finances them with loans. In case of a default, the investors have access to real estate or other assets which they could sell to cover their losses.

Yet another group selects scalable impact enterprises and invests equity to cover the risks of the business models. They support the companies with their network and guidance. There are differences in how the investors select the companies. Some are willing to accept lower returns if the impact is higher, while others would accept social returns but are not willing to pay for it.

The discussion above has shown how diverse the sector is and what kind of considerations have to be taken into account to analyze impact enterprises and identify suitable investment targets.

There is a long history of research focused on the identification of selection criteria for venture capital funds. In the impact investing area, selection criteria are different (Achleitner et al. 2013; Achleitner, Heister, and Spiess-Knafl 2014). Investors analyze the entrepreneur or the founding team, the financials, the business model, the stakeholder, and the delivery model or the impact model, among others. There are many conflicting views on how to think about return expectations in this space. Some say that high social impact leads to high financial returns (Grabenwarter and Liechtenstein 2011). Others would argue that it is the other way round as higher impact leads to lower financial returns.

This helps to explain the difficulties in predicting which companies will be successful in the future. First, it is necessary to understand what drives success. It is not really easy to understand why certain start-ups succeed while others fail. Some mention the soft factors as more relevant and focus on the team, the founder personality, or the culture.

As a second step, it would be necessary to have a relatively complete and consistent dataset of data points for each company. Some only have a pitch deck with a narrative and only a few numbers to crunch. In some cases, it might not even make sense if there are no revenues to analyze.

In some cases, it will take up to ten years to determine which companies are successful. However, the label "success" is necessary to train the model on the data.

Notes

1 For more information, see https://demyst.com/ and www.accion.org/how-we-work/inv est/accion-venture-lab#portfolio
2 For more information, see www.safaricom.co.ke/personal/m-pesa
3 For more information, see www.accion.org/fintech-start-up-destacame-closes-seed-fund ing-round-to-expand-access-to-credit-in-latin-america and www.accion.org/destacame-chile-alternative-data. www.destacame.cl/
4 For more information, see https://karmalife.ai
5 For more information, see www.indicina.co/
6 For more information, see https://aquaconnect.blue/

5

BASIC PRINCIPLES OF THE BLOCKCHAIN TECHNOLOGY

5.1   How to think about the blockchain technology

Non-fungible tokens (NFTs), cryptocurrencies, crypto assets, and its underlying blockchain technology are often the results of heated discussions. Some critics say that there is no real use case for the blockchain technology, while others see a future completely built on blockchain applications.

There are many perspectives from which to consider blockchain or distributed ledger technology (DLT). Cryptographers and mathematicians might love the clever way of securing information. Economists can spend weeks arguing about the role and volatility of cryptocurrencies. Anarchists love the independence from public authorities. Market theorists regularly identify new models.

There are different ways to think about the blockchain technology. A few examples might be helpful to understand the opportunities, the main principles, as well as the limitations.

The first example is the use of ledgers in our daily lives.

Imagine that you want to transfer a certain amount of capital to a family member. You would go to a bank and tell the bank that they should transfer a certain sum from your bank account to the bank account of your family member. It means your account is reduced for a specific sum which is added to the bank account of your family member.

All transactions of a bank are stored and managed in a central ledger. Keeping the ledger secure is a key priority for the bank, and a loss of the central ledger would be catastrophic. Even in civil war areas, banks are usually able to maintain records of their bank accounts.

The trusted and centralized party which is managing transactions is a recurring theme over time. In the past, temples or civil servants kept track of transactions, and it is not without reason that some of the earliest writings were basically transaction records (Friberg 1984).

DOI: 10.4324/9781003218913-5

In general, there are an almost endless number of ledgers. National public authorities document and record property rights and also enforce them if necessary. Ledger maintained by the public authorities proves if a person is born, alive, or dead. It also records citizen rights connected to nationalities. For example, it makes a difference if persons are traveling with a North Korean, Canadian, or Brazilian passport in terms of travel restrictions. Voting rights are also tied to nationalities or residence rights.

Not only public authorities maintain a ledger. For example, fitness studios, country clubs, or theaters all have ledgers with an overview of its member or clients. Ledgers are thus a central part of our lives.

The blockchain technology is also called DLT and hints at the fact that it is eliminating the central ledger and puts the information across many different ledgers. The main idea is that many different individuals are observing and documenting the transactions for the entire network.

The blockchain technology can also help to secure assets as one of the key problems of digital assets is the problem of double spending (Chohan 2021). Double spending means that any person holding digital assets could spend them more than once. The question remains how you can make sure that each asset is owned and spent only once. That is where consensus mechanisms become relevant.

One could imagine a village in which every member notices if a cow is given to a certain person for a certain occasion. The village members would be able to document the transfer of a cow, grain, or other goods. This is what happens on the Micronesian island of Yap. They have an unusual form of currency which takes the form of human-sized discs of rock. The interesting part is that the so-called Rai were often too large to transport, and there was a need for a consensus mechanism to establish who owned which stones. The consensus mechanism was an oral record of the ownership (Gentle 2021). Interestingly, this oral recording also enabled to keep the value of the stones which were lost at sea (Gilliland 1975).

Whenever someone transfers capital or any other goods, this transfer is thus documented across all ledgers. The next step is to make sure that everyone has the same information, and nobody is tampering with the data. A single person might manipulate the data and give additional capital to a single person. You might possibly add another 0 to your bank account. To eliminate this possibility, there needs to be a consensus mechanism for all stakeholders to make sure that there is the same information and ground truth for all participants of the network.

These mechanisms open a wide design space. For example, they enable the secure and permanent storage of information for instances where information needs to be stored permanently. Consider the cases of land registry, vaccinations, or service delivery where the blockchain technology enables the storage of any kind of digital information securely and permanently. There is no way to change information linked to the blockchain.

The blockchain technology can also guarantee that the code is running as designed and never changes. Kewell, Adams, and Parry (2017) summarize it as "code substitutes for trust." The technology thus enables algorithmically controlled systems. Blockchain-run models allow anyone to specify that a transfer of a certain amount happens on certain data dependent on certain criteria defined beforehand. Consider the case of disaster relief where cash is disbursed once an earthquake happens. Instead of human oversight, there is an algorithm that oversees transactions, and nobody can interfere with the fundamental aspects of the business model.

Trust in the social economy is mostly built on local networks and personal relationships. There might be some exceptions, such as with highly reputable international organizations like the Red Cross or Amnesty International. Blockchain technology can create the trust which is necessary to implement certain models. The creation of trust is surely undermined by fraudulent business models or statements that have been wildly overblown. Some projects which have been implemented were either nonsensical or just schemes to extract value from the wider (social) economy.

These perspectives of secure storage and algorithmic governance have opened a new space for designs and led to a proliferation of new business models. Underlying all these concepts is a strong culture and community. Already Swan (2015) outlined the specific culture. It is a space full of references, abbreviations, and memes which are rarely understandable for those outside of the community. This strong sense of community also supported the long-term growth and resilience of the ecosystem.

The interest in the blockchain technology seems to be correlated with the price of Bitcoin. Each time Bitcoin hits a new high, there is a wave of start-up activity.

The last years have seen cycles of hype and bust. The first cycle was in the years from 2009 to 2012. This was the period when much of the underlying infrastructure was created. The second cycle followed in the years from 2012 to 2016 and saw the creation of the Ethereum blockchain, which drove much of the subsequent growth. The third cycle ran from 2016 to 2019 and saw a broad set of implementations (Dixon and Lazzarin 2020). It is a bit too early to clearly identify the fourth wave, but the period from 2020 to 2022 saw a range of policy actions and widespread acceptance as an institutional asset class.

The adoption rate of the blockchain technology across industries has been significant. There are now examples of its use in agriculture, logistics, and financial services, built around storing information. It also helps that millennials are at ease with the technology.

The blockchain technology offers and enables some key benefits. It is fully transparent, respects the privacy of individuals, and there are no ways to tamper with the data. The blockchain is thus a single source of truth and can help to solve the two questions below:

- How can you make sure that everyone has access to the same information?
- How can you create a dataset where no one knows any other person and still believes in the accuracy of the information?

There are little opportunities for individuals to transact when they do not trust one another. Trust is a key principle of the blockchain technology. The question is how individuals and organizations can create trust and a reputation. It is usually created by establishing a track record of actions which were in line with the expectations of the stakeholders.

This is also the core of an argument proposed by Andolfatto (2018). The information about a single event might not be interesting, but a chain of events might create meaningful information. Examples are the information about vehicle safety inspections, trainings, or loan repayment data. A bank might reasonably believe that someone who has a longer history of repaying loans might be in a better position.

Andolfatto (2018) also raises the point that a blockchain is a form of history by recording events of the past. The recording of events is a privilege in itself and should be kept in mind when analyzing networks.

5.2   Definition of the blockchain technology

There are various definitions to define a blockchain.

Wood (2014) defines a blockchain-based system as "a cryptographically secure, transaction-based state machine." This definition already includes the relevant aspects such as security, cryptography, or the focus on transactions.

Rauchs et al. (2018) collect a number of definitions for distributed ledger technologies.

The terms DLT and blockchain technology are often used synonymously. Distributed ledger technologies include all technologies which aim to make distributed ledgers work. Blockchain technologies are a subset of the distributed ledger technologies based on a specific form of consensus building.

One of the common themes is the degree of the centralization. A fully centralized system is controlled by a single entity or person, whereas a fully decentralized system has no central controlling entity or person and works on an established coordination system.

The choice of the system always comes with a number of implications (Rauchs et al. 2018). A fully centralized system is very efficient as it has a high throughput capacity and low overhead expenses. However, the controlling entity or person can always change the content of the database and exercise censorship. Such a system requires a high degree of trust from its stakeholders. Private blockchains follow a more centralized approach and restrict reading and writing privileges for a certain group of participants.

A fully decentralized system might have a much lower throughput capacity, but it can also be called a trustless system. There is also a high censorship resistance. Fully decentralized systems have an open-source approach and usually an egalitarian philosophy (Seyedsayamdost and Vanderwal, 2020). Everyone can access and build tools on top of a decentralized blockchain system. Traditional databases are relatively easy and cost-efficient to operate but this does not apply to blockchain-based databases.

TABLE 5.1 Definitions for DLT

Definition	Source
a specific implementation of the broader category of 'shared ledgers', which are simply defined as a shared record of data across different parties	Natarajan, Krause, and Gradstein (2017)
technology that 'allow[s] their users to store and access information relating to a given set of assets and their holders in a shared database of either transactions or account balances'. This information is distributed among users, who could then use it to settle their transfers of, e.g., securities and cash, without needing to rely on a trusted central validation system	Pinna and Ruttenberg (2016)
distributed, cryptographically secure, and cryptoeconomically incentivized consensus engine	Davidson, De Filippi, and Potts (2016)
A DLT is a distributed database, in the sense that each node has a synchronized copy of the data but departs from the traditional distributed database architectures in three important ways: (i) decentralization; (ii) reliability in trustless environments; (iii) cryptographic encryption. The Bank of England summarizes its definition as: 'a database architecture which enables the keeping and sharing of records in a distributed and decentralised way, while ensuring its integrity through the use of consensus-based validation protocols and cryptographic signatures'	Benos, Garratt, and Gurrola-Perez (2017)
DLT has established itself as an umbrella term to designate multiparty systems that operate in an environment with no central operator or authority, despite parties who may be unreliable or malicious ('adversarial environment'). Blockchain technology is often considered a specific subset of the broader DLT universe that uses a particular data structure consisting of a chain of hash-linked blocks of data.	Rauchs et al. (2018)

Source: Own illustration.

5.3 History and evolving narratives

The basis of the blockchain technology has already been developed in the 1980s and 1990s. Historical accounts of the blockchain technology and its use usually start with the paper titled "Bitcoin: A Peer-to-Peer Electronic Cash System" published by Satoshi Nakamoto (2008). Others highlight the characters of the people which were attracted by anonymity, academic novelty, or the economics of cryptocurrencies (Mezrich 2019).

Bitcoin was first introduced in a white paper in 2008 and promised digital cash which is untraceable but fully secured by the underlying algorithm. It was also the time of the financial crisis, and it was conceptually seen as a way to facilitate transactions between individuals without relying on central third parties.

In the early years where only Bitcoin was available, the first miners and exchanges started their operations. Bitcoin wallets have also been developed. There was a strong narrative around the use of Bitcoin as an alternative currency and payment system. The idea of digital cash for regular and recurring payments has not been found to be efficient as transaction costs remain relatively high. It is still difficult to find retailers which accept cryptocurrencies as a form of payment.

Perdana et al. (2021) find that media reports in the early years were often related to dubious transactions. Silk Road, dark web, and drug payments were early use cases. Media report often covered the idea of a currency. The collapse of the exchange Mt. Gox was also covered in the media.

Another aspect was the near collapse of the Cyprus economy and the banking crisis. In 2013, Cyprus faced a collapsing banking industry and had to accept a major bailout for a recapitalization. One part of the agreement was that depositors had to contribute to the savings of the banks. The contribution depended on the deposit balance, but some faced levies up to 50%. The realization that bank deposits are not as safe as initially thought was beneficial for Bitcoin and led to increased downloads for the apps (Luther and Salter 2017). This helps to explain why the blockchain technology is a favorite tool for libertarians who strongly oppose strong government intervention.

In 2015, there was a wave related to new fundraising tools which saw the blockchain technology as an approach to raise and allocate capital. It was in line with the idea that cryptocurrencies are a store of value.

The second wave was significantly influenced by the launch of Ethereum. New blockchains were invented and alternative coins added. It was also the period of the Initial Coin Offering (ICOs). Perdana et al. (2021) find the first mentions of smart contracts and the discussion of electronic health records. This points toward a broadening of the field and the concept.

Starting in 2017, there was a new narrative which saw the blockchain technology as a new institutional asset class. It was also seen as a hedge against central bank's monetary policy and as a hedge against a potential government collapse. Perdana et al. (2021) find in their media analysis that financial services are more widely discussed starting in 2017. There were also more mentions related to business or industry.

The third wave was mostly related to the development of decentralized finance. There were also more apps and the first marketplaces related to NFTs. In general, these waves are tied to the development of the Bitcoin price as there is a relationship between the price, general public interest, and developer activities.

5.4 Technology and ecosystem

The components of the blockchain technology are relatively old. Most of the key ideas have been developed in the 1980s and 1990s (Narayanan and Clark 2017). There were a few technologies which needed to be linked:

- Linked timestamping, verifiable logs
- Digital cash

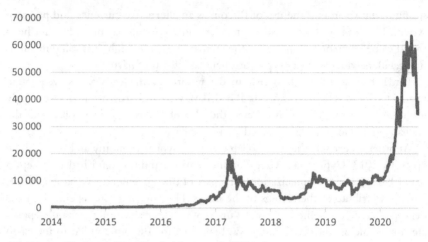

FIGURE 5.1 Closing daily price development of Bitcoin

Source: Own illustration based on publicly available data

- Proof of work
- Byzantine fault tolerance
- Public keys as identities
- Smart contracts

Researchers began publishing on these topics in the 1980s and 1990s. Satoshi Nakamoto who invented Bitcoin by writing the white paper was putting together existing ideas and concepts to develop a new model.

There are different layers which make up the blockchain ecosystem (e.g., Schär 2021). They are often used in different versions and with changing terminologies.

The first and most basic layer is the consensus or settlement layer and consists of the blockchain itself. The Ethereum blockchain or the Bitcoin blockchain are among the best known. A native asset is the primary digital asset of the system. These are used to pay transaction fees or structure how information is recorded. For example, the Ether (ETH) token is the primary token for the Ethereum blockchain.

On an almost weekly basis, new blockchains are introduced which promise lower fees and higher throughputs. One of the latest announcements was Espresso Systems which has raised $32 million and describes its approach as "a layer 1 blockchain system that combines proof-of-stake consensus and a ZK-Rollup mechanism to achieve high throughput and low fees."[1]

The next layer is the asset layer which consists of the thousands of tokens which are issued on a specific blockchain. At the moment, most tokens are issued on the Ethereum blockchain. The protocol layer includes the set of smart contracts which are enabling exchanges or lending protocols such as Maker or Uniswap. The application layer is the user interface and enables easy interaction with the protocols.

TABLE 5.2 Actor types found in the ecosystem

Developers	Administrators	Gateways	Participants
Core protocol	Foundation	Gatekeeper	Auditor
Client	Company	Oracle	Record producer
Application	Consortia	Custodian	Lightweight client
External systems	Open-source Community	Issuer	End user
		Exchange	

Source: Rauchs et al. (2018).

One key element of the blockchain industry is the existence of vibrant ecosystems. There are various actors in the ecosystem (Rauchs et al. 2018).

Developers are writing and reviewing the code. They need to make sure that the core protocol and all the interfaces and applications and links to external systems are working. Open-source communities are often heavily involved in these developments.

Administrators control access to the platform. There are various forms of how this can be structured. Gateways are the bridge or link between the system and the environment. There are oracles, gatekeepers, or exchanges which take on this role. Participants are miners, users, and auditors.

5.5 Consensus mechanisms

The blockchain technology can be described as a record-keeping system which stores the same information in different locations. At the core of the blockchain technology is the consensus mechanism which ensures that everyone has access to the same information at the same time. The underlying technology guarantees it, and there is no necessity for additional actors to take over this role.

Andolfatto (2018) puts trust and reputation at the center of conventional protocols outside of the blockchain technology for achieving this consensus. It is time-consuming to build a good reputation and economic actors do not want to put their reputation at risk for short-term gains.

The blockchain technology is basically an approach to remove the trust requirement and set up a trustless protocol. There needs to be some instance which verifies and collects all transactions, and various methods can be used to achieve this consensus (Tasca and Tessone, 2018).

The most prominent consensus mechanism is proof of work. So-called miners are solving a complicated mathematical equation. Those which solve the equation can add the next block and receive a reward. The reward is currently valued at 6.25 BTC for Bitcoin (equivalent to $260,000 as of March 2022) roughly every 10 minutes. In the Ethereum network, it takes only a few seconds until a new block is added. The daily block rewards amount to 13,500 ETC (equivalent to $39.3 million per day) which is comparable to the block rewards for Bitcoin.

In addition to the block rewards, there is typically a fee to transact or use the blockchain to store information. For example, in the Ethereum blockchain, this fee is called gas. Users can determine a gas price and a gas limit to represent how much they are willing to pay miners for the transaction.

Transaction fees are necessary as every operation is recorded by every miner in the network. The user is thus paying to store his information on as many computers as possible. This is also the reason why smart contracts are structured in such a way that can be programmed with a few lines of code. The transaction fees are also meant to prevent an overuse of the network.

Another consensus mechanism is proof of stake and is a reaction to the substantial accusations Bitcoin and Ethereum have faced over the last years for their electricity consumption. Some projects have tried to use the computing power for scientific purposes (e.g., Primecoin). For example, Bitcoin consumes the equivalent of Finland or Washington State for the maintenance of the blockchain (Huang, O'Neill, and Tabuchi 2021).

The main idea is that it is necessary to hold a stake of the digital assets to be allowed to write on the blockchain. There is also an incentive alignment. It would make little sense to corrupt a blockchain if the attacker himself suffers economic losses. It works in a way that the miners in the network are randomly selected to add the next block to the blockchain and are rewarded for adding the block. One of the more prominent models is the Cardano blockchain which is using the proof-of-stake mechanism (Kiayias et al., 2017).

Other concepts include proof of authority, proof of capacity, proof of burn, and hybrid concepts. Proof of authority can be seen in private networks where some authorities can allow other entities to add content to the blockchain. Proof of capacity is a concept where the miner needs to show that they reserve memory. Proof of burn is an interesting element where miners are burning digital assets. We can also expect other consensus mechanisms to emerge in the future.

5.6 Cryptographic components

A few components make up the blockchain technology, whereof cryptography is the most important one.

Cryptography has a long history. One of the first cryptographic tools was used by Caesar and was basically a shift in the alphabet. A "b" became a "d" and an "m" became an "o." These relatively simple methods were soon developed further.

Symmetric cryptography was found to be insecure as the keys for encrypting are the same as those for decrypting. In asymmetric cryptography, it is more difficult as the keys for locking are different from the keys for unlocking. These asymmetric keys are the foundation for the blockchain technology.

Hashes are another core feature of the blockchain technology. Any sentence or number can be transformed in a hash. The two examples show the mechanism and the difficulty in reversing the hash function.

TABLE 5.3 Block information

Hash	0000000000000000000013632337fcdacb17d030b0f93bba5b4 29a68478385130
Timestamp	2022-02-10 18:51
Height	722648
Miner	AntPool
Number of transactions	2,909
Difficulty	26,690,525,287,405.50
Merkle root	4022463188a3ec5fe831004da94644e5255dee27b01c4be77bf8a 95d84cf6b73
Nonce	3,517,233,304
Transaction volume	39035.75642558 BTC
Block reward	6.25000000 BTC
Fee reward	0.22414914 BTC

Source: Blockchain.com (2022).

> Sentence: This is Example A.
> Hash: 42a21f5f7b5f67d21b040d97a7afcfba
> Sentence: This is Example B.
> Hash: 673f93d476c6e692c072e46dc909e0c8

Each block as shown in the table above has a number of information. It contains the block headers, information about the set of transactions, and information about the validity of the transactions.

For example, the Block 722648 was mined on February 10, 2022. The miner of this block received a reward of 6.25 Bitcoin which had a value of $275,000. This is called the base reward. Moreover, the miner received an additional 0.22 Bitcoin as fee for the execution of the 2,909 transactions.

5.7   Smart contracts

Contracts are a key element of economic theories and are an important reason why firms exist in the first place. Coase (1937) wrote about the theory of firm and put transaction costs at the center of the theory and influenced decades of academic research. In principle, it is possible to contract everything on the market. The emergence of the internet and the platform economy with crowdwork has dramatically reduced the costs of identifying workers and contracting work. Complete contracts are clearly defined for each scenario. However, they can only be found in rather narrow settings and environments.

Transaction costs might lead to the decision that work should be done inside an organization, firm, or other business entity. The agency theory is based on considerations of what happens when not everything can be regulated or foreseen with contracts (Jensen and Meckling 1976). Not every scenario can be described and steps foreseen. This is the reason why incomplete contracts are the usual form of contracts.

Given that contracts are almost always incomplete, it is more complicated to set up smart contracts. For example, there are always uncertainties such as what happens when a pandemic or a war breaks out.

Digital tools have helped to reduce transaction costs quite significantly. Reasons are that platforms help to reduce search and transaction costs. For example, it is now possible to find a designer in Bangladesh or Pakistan for a fraction of the costs it costs to employ designers in the United States.

Smart contracts are basically an algorithm which is executed when certain requirements are met. It is a form of "If-Then-Statement." Smart contracts as a term have been coined by Nick Szabo (1994).

Below is an example for the code of a smart contract (Ethereum 2022). It shows that they are just a few lines of code to operate a smart contract for operating a vending machine.

```solidity
1    pragma solidity 0.8.7;
2
3    contract VendingMachine {
4
5        // Declare state variables of the contract
6        address public owner;
7        mapping (address => uint) public cupcakeBalances;
8
9        // When 'VendingMachine' contract is deployed:
10       // 1. set the deploying address as the owner of the contract
11       // 2. set the deployed smart contract's cupcake balance to 100
12       constructor() {
13           owner = msg.sender;
14           cupcakeBalances[address(this)] = 100;
15       }
16
17       // Allow the owner to increase the smart contract's cupcake balance
18       function refill(uint amount) public {
19           require(msg.sender == owner, "Only the owner can refill.");
20           cupcakeBalances[address(this)] += amount;
21       }
22
23       // Allow anyone to purchase cupcakes
24       function purchase(uint amount) public payable {
25           require(msg.value >= amount * 1 ether, "You must pay at least 1 ETH per cupcake");
26           require(cupcakeBalances[address(this)] >= amount, "Not enough cupcakes in stock to complete this purchase");
```

```
27        cupcakeBalances[address(this)] -= amount;
28        cupcakeBalances[msg.sender] += amount;
29    }
30  }
31
```

It is necessary to keep smart contracts simple as every additional line increases the transaction fees for the execution of its services.

5.8 Tokens

Tokens are a key element in the blockchain environment. Oliveira et al. (2018) define eight different token archetypes. Each token has a different function.

The distinction between some of the tokens might not be too clear. For example, there will surely be overlaps between the equity token and the funding token.

To further detail the characteristics and features, Ankenbrand et al. (2020) propose an asset taxonomy which can be used for crypto as well as non-crypto assets. They discuss the different features listed below.

TABLE 5.4 Token archetypes

Archetype	Main Purposes	Description
Cryptocurrency	Currency	A token with the ambition to become a widespread digital form of currency.
Equity token	Earnings, store of wealth	A token which confers to its holder a right to equity-related earnings, such as profit sharing, application rents, or platform fees.
Funding token	Store of wealth, funding	A token which is perceived as a long-term investment from the holder's perspective and as a financing vehicle for the project's team and/or the community (bounties).
Consensus token	Validation, reward, store of wealth	A token which is used as a reward to nodes which ensure data validation and consensus.
Work token	Work rewards	A token which is used as reward to users who complete certain actions or exhibit certain behavior.
Voting token	Voting right	A token which confers a voting right to its holder.
Asset token	Voting right, asset ownership	A token which represents asset ownership.
Payment token	Payment	A token which is used as internal payment method in the application.

Source: Based on Oliveira et al. (2018).

- claim structure,
- the technology,
- underlying or collateral,
- consensus or validation mechanism,
- legal status,
- governance,
- information complexity,
- legal structure,
- information interface,
- total supply,
- issuance,
- redemption,
- transferability and
- fungibility.

The claim structure is well known from financial instruments. There could be no claim, a flexible claim, or a fixed claim. A flexible claim is dependent on certain triggers or changes. For example, dividend payments will generally depend on the profits of a company.

The asset can exist in a physical form, a digital form such as electronic shares or based on the blockchain technology. This tokenization has also received regulatory attention over the last years (Nassr 2021).

The underlying of the token is usually the driver of the value, although there might be none for most of the cryptocurrencies. For other cryptographic assets, it might be a token representing something valuable within the blockchain context. Ankenbrand et al. (2020) add companies, bankable assets, tangible assets, or contracts as further examples.

Another element of the taxonomy is the mechanism to achieve consensus or validate the agreement. The instant finality is achieved with notary services of signed contracts. The blockchain types of consensuses discussed above have a probabilistic finality. That means that there is a high probability of finality which increases further over time.

Some assets such as loans, mortgages, equity shares, or insurance claims are tightly regulated. Other assets are unregulated in the sense that there are no regulatory requirements.

The governance of the asset can either be centralized or decentralized. A centralized governance relies on a stock exchange, platform, or similar organizations while decentralized governance can mainly be found in the blockchain environment. Lately, there have been many discussions on the centralization of certain elements as many parts of the Web3 environments are still highly centralized.

Ankenbrand et al. (2020) also discuss the information complexity associated with the asset. The first category is related to specific values such as commodity prices or currencies. The second category of assets is related to contracts which determine the payment structures. They define the third category as those which are based on universally programmable computational models such as Ethereum.

The legal structure is also a key element in classifying assets. There might be no legal structure governing the asset. Other legal structures include foundations, bonds, shares, or other alternative legal structures.

The next design element is the information interface and the question how the owner receives or sends relevant information. There might be no interface, a qualitative interface or a quantitative interface. A qualitative interface could be a general assembly, while a quantitative interface might be an oracle in a blockchain context.

Assets in general usually have a certain limit. There are only a certain number of equity shares or a certain amount of gold. The total supply of assets might be fixed such as in the case of the Bitcoin. It might be managed flexibly by authorized parties or conditional upon certain predefined criteria.

Closely related to the supply is the question how the asset is generated and how the number of outstanding assets can be reduced if necessary. Assets could be generated and reduced conditionally or flexibly. There might also be the case of fixed or even no schedule for the reduction of assets.

Ankenbrand et al. (2020) also include the features of transferability and fungibility. Transferability refers to the question if the asset can be transferred to another person or not. Most assets are transferable except if they are somehow tied to a person. The fungibility will be discussed in more detail for the NFTs, but it refers to the question if an asset can be interchanged with another asset of the same type. Especially artwork is not considered to be fungible as each piece is unique.

A special category is NFTs. They have been featured widely and have been traded for high amounts. In principle, they try to solve a specific problem. One of the problems with the current social media platforms is that files are uploaded to the platform, and ownership and monetization rights are transferred to these companies. There is an endless stream of digital creativity which is transferred free of charge to internet companies which profit from these assets.

The blockchain technology can ensure public access to a digital file and ensure that the private ownership remains traceable. An NFT is a token with a unique identifier and some metadata. The metadata might include aspects such as the creation date or the price history.

There are also so-called social tokens. The Cedar Coin developed by the UNDP Lebanon is an example for a social token.[2] Individuals can buy a Cedar Coin and have a proof of planting. Cedar Coins are more of a recognition tool, and there is no market or other value beyond reputational gains.

In some concepts individuals create personal tokens and sell them in promise for something in exchange. For example, there are coins minted by artists and by entrepreneurs.

There are also experiments where access to certain groups and newsletters is only available with a certain amount of tokens. Again, it is another example, where service providers provide a wide range of tools to control access, create tokens, and other services.

Notes

1 For more information, see www.espressosys.com/
2 For more information, see www.cedarcoin.org/about-us

6
BLOCKCHAIN-ENABLED IMPACT BUSINESS MODELS

6.1 Introduction

The blockchain technology opens a rich design space. The main feature of this design space is the potential to combine economic incentives, algorithmic commitments, and payments in an accountable, secure, and verifiable environment. In addition, all features are instantaneous, and there are no losses of trust. Smart contracts are the basis for the emerging business models.

Zahra et al. (2009) introduced the "social engineer" in their typology of social entrepreneurs. This might also be a good category for those types of examples we see in the blockchain space. It is often about finding solutions for problems which should also consider existing social practices and needs.

There is a large community of people who claim to develop "blockchain for good" each with different motivations (Coppi 2021). Some see the unbanked populations as a business opportunity to explore, while others are working hard to improve the living conditions of individuals. Overall, many projects claiming to improve society are merely marketing slogans without substance.

Drivers to implement blockchain solutions include accountability, visibility, traceability, or efficiency, among others. However, there are also barriers including a lack of technical skills and training, privacy concerns, or governance challenges (Baharmand, Maghsoudi, and Coppi 2021).

Blockchain-based concepts are eliminating the need for intermediaries which are often local banks in the Global South. Seyedsayamdost and Vanderwal (2020) rightly point out that the technology has been created and is mainly used in the industrial countries.

There is the idea that there are different eras related to the history of the internet and that the blockchain technology is at the core of a new generation of business models.

DOI: 10.4324/9781003218913-6

Web 1.0 includes those websites which provided information in the form of information, e-mail, and directories and only needed low bandwidth. Examples include Google, Amazon, or other retailers. Web 2.0 includes those services which are based on broadband access, social aspects, and cloud computing. Gig economy marketplaces would be summarized in this category. Web 3.0 includes the crypto space, internet of things, or aspects related to 5G.

It is also interesting to note how business models are developing. At the beginning, it was mostly about rebuilding existing models and somehow connecting them to a blockchain. Swan (2015) lists 84 different options for business models which are all based on existing options. It was collected by a venture capital fund and is interesting insofar as the ideas only tried to replicate or decentralize existing business models. In many cases, it was not promising as those ideas already worked well, and decentralization only adds costs.

TABLE 6.1 List of blockchain-based ideas in the early stages of the development

Category	Potential Applications
Financial instruments, records, and models	Currency, private equities, public equities, bonds, derivatives (futures, forwards, swaps, options, and more complex variations), voting rights associated with any of the proceeding, commodities, spending records, trading records, mortgage/loan records, servicing records, crowdfunding, microfinance, micro-charity
Public records	Land titles, vehicle registries, business license, business incorporation/dissolution records, business ownership records, regulatory records, criminal records, passports, birth certificates, death certificates, voter IDs, voting, health/safety inspections, building permits, gun permits, forensic evidence, court records, voting records, nonprofit records, government/nonprofit accounting/transparency
Private records	Contracts, signatures, wills, trusts, escrows, GPS trails (personal)
Other semipublic records	Degree, certification, learning outcomes, grades, HR records, medical records, accounting records, business transaction records, genome data, GPS trails (institutional), delivery records, arbitration
Physical asset keys	Home / apartment keys, vacation home / timeshare keys, hotel room keys, car keys, rental car keys, leased cars keys, locker keys, safety deposit box keys, package delivery, betting records, fantasy sports records
Intangibles	Coupons, vouchers, reservations, movie tickets, patents, copyrights, trademarks, software licenses, videogame licenses, music/movie/book licenses, domain names, online identities, proof of authorship/proof of prior art
Other	Documentary records (photos, audio, video), data records (sports scores, temperature), Sim cards, GPS network identity, gun unlock codes, weapons unlock codes, nuclear launch codes, spam control (micropayments for posting)

Source: Based on Swan (2015).

The blockchain technology can store information of any kind. It can be information about future payments, contractual agreements, or just fingerprints for certain transactions.

Some are referring in discussions to the term "cryptoeconomics" to hint at the fact that economics and cryptographic principles are combined. It also highlights the aspect of money as an engineering problem.

The whole system is built on rewards and sanctions. Miners are rewarded for their work guaranteeing the consensus and integrity of the underlying information. Every transaction on the blockchain can be checked and traced virtually. This helps to reduce information asymmetry.

However, there are some downsides to this total transparency. For example, individuals should be able to hide payments related to mental health treatments or the support of opposition groups. This might lead to real-life effects for those individuals.

In principle, participants are completely anonymous, but there are many cases where individuals could be linked to certain wallets. Some of the new blockchains are also putting an emphasis on a privacy layer to protect the legitimate interests of individuals and organizations.

6.2 Identification of good projects

Coppi (2021) proposes four criteria to assess if a certain project can be considered good.

* Solidity
* Delivery
* Scope
* Governance

It means that there should be a development team; a delivery of products; its scope should be in line with social objectives; and there should be a governance system which controls the management, maintenance, and delivery of the products. It is indeed the case that many projects only use some vocabulary to make their projects sound good.[1]

Pschetz et al. (2020) discuss how a potential project aiming for social impact should be designed. In general, there are different steps. Social impact is always related to improving the lives of individuals, and mostly, it is concerned with local needs. Local target groups usually have very different needs. In their study of Jamaican farmers, Pschetz et al. (2020) find a number of issues farmers are facing. Payments are often delayed, and farmers have no information about the demand from hotels which are a good source of demand driven by sustainable tourism requirements. Another issue is that farmers have no access to credit from financial institutions.

Agricultural products are hard to track, and there are a number of information management problems (Griffin et al. 2021). These problems include messy farm data, uncertain data quality, resource tracking, and supply chain coordination.

TABLE 6.2 Tendencies and characteristics of the blockchain technology and their potential benefits and challenges to agricultural stakeholders

Tendencies	Characteristics	Benefits and Challenges to Agricultural Stakeholders
Disintermediation	Decentralization: With no central authority, distributed ledger technologies (DLTs) are run by peers who don't necessarily know each other. Consensus (or rules to verify, validate, and add transactions) is defined a priori.	Benefits: Disintermediation could support smallholder farmers to guarantee better share of profit for their produce. Challenges: Creation of new forms of intermediation, job losses.
Trustless exchanges	Digital signatures: Messages encrypted with a public key can only be decrypted by a specified recipient using a private key. This ensures that transactions originate from the right person and cannot be accessed or modified by others.	Benefits: Guarantee that an exchange (e.g., future monetary transaction) will take place regardless of the levels of trust between parties. Challenges: Anonymity.
Durable, secure decentralized networks	Replication: All nodes or participants have a copy of the blockchain ledger. These are constantly updated and validated in the network. Unlike centralized systems, there is no single point of failure.	Benefits: Security of data sets. Replication of files distribute power between peers, since all of them own the data, this could in theory facilitate bottom-up governance. Challenges: Could prevent public oversight.
Transparency and immutability	Immutability of records: The way each transaction is cryptographically recorded on the blockchain, and then validated through consensus, makes it nearly impossible to make changes to the ledger without detection. In this sense, records are irreversible and tamper-proof.	Benefits: Digital scarcity can create new forms of value. Immutability of records could provide more trust in the recorded information, e.g., regarding the origin of produce. Information can be made public by default (transparency). Challenges: Strike a balance between personal privacy and inability to delete data from ledgers.

TABLE 6.2 (Cont.)

Tendencies	Characteristics	Benefits and Challenges to Agricultural Stakeholders
Maintenance of high-quality accurate data	Time-stamping: Transactions are time-stamped. Data such as details about payments, contract, transfer of ownership, etc. are linked publicly and immutably to a certain data and time. No one is able to modify what has been recorded and time-stamped.	Benefits: Support record keeping and information sharing. Here too the system could potentially provide more reliability in data provision. Challenges: Access to personal information, privacy.
Automation of predetermined protocols	Smart contracts: are tamper-proof algorithms that execute "if-then" instructions: "if" something happens, "then" certain transactions or actions are done. This way, transactions can be automatically executed without human intervention.	Benefits: Guarantee that predetermined prices and conditions (e.g., defined to protect farmers) are met. Challenges: Potential to bypass local authorities and regulations.

Source: Based on Pschetz et al. (2020).

6.3 Markets, institutions, and organizational forms

Social business models are usually related to markets which do not work properly. Markets balance supply and demand where more demand will lead to higher prices and consequently to more supply.

This sounds rather straightforward, but markets fail regularly. The markets for theater productions, affordable housing, or renewable energy are far from perfect. The failure to supply products and services is the main reason that social business models are needed. Much of the academic literature focused on the design of blockchain systems is related to mechanism design (Ast and Deffains 2021).

The traditional view is that institutions and organizations are necessary to coordinate economic activities. Ostrom (2009) defines institutions broadly as

> the prescriptions that humans use to organize all forms of repetitive and structured interactions including those within families, neighborhoods, markets, firms, sports leagues, churches, private associations, and governments at all scales. Individuals interacting within rule-structured situations face choices regarding the actions and strategies they take, leading to consequences for themselves and for others.

It is in line with other researchers who find that institutions are relevant in every context and every country (Mair, Marti, and Ventresca 2012).

The protocols in the blockchain space usually start with entrepreneurs who have an idea and work out how a mechanism or game should be designed (Ast and Deffains 2021). In the process, they build an institution to coordinate economic and noneconomic activities. This is comparable to mechanism design for social goals (Maskin 2008).

Another element is what is called blockchain guarantees (Kaal 2020). Every participant in the system has the guarantee that nobody will change the code and its intended operations.

In capitalist societies, it is often assumed that the only legal form are privately-run enterprises. However, there are also cooperatives, nonprofit organizations, or associations. They all share participatory decision-making processes and inclusive ownership or no ownership at all.

The blockchain technology enables new forms of organizations which are run algorithmically and can implement hybrid forms as well. Hybrid organizations are becoming increasingly important. They follow not only commercial logics but also incorporate institutional logics from other fields.

Family firms incorporate socio-emotional wealth considerations (Berrone et al. 2010). Green companies incorporate environmental considerations. Political companies follow political preferences in employing as many people as possible or enabling corruption. Social enterprises incorporate social sector logics (Pache and Santos 2013).

Hybridity is thus an integrative strategy and combines different logics in one organization. It also enables new business models. The reputation of family firms is a signaling factor. Social enterprises can use resources or pricing strategies which might not be available to other companies (Spiess-Knafl, Mast, and Jansen 2015).

Impact-oriented enterprises face problems which are different in every jurisdiction and sometimes even at regional levels. They are thus in a setting where they need to integrate divergent views in their organization. Hybridity can be seen as a necessary feature of the business model. Hybrid organizations are difficult to understand from the outside and inherently more complex to scale. Stakeholder management necessitates more attention from the social enterprise.

The hybrid nature also makes it necessary to build trust. At a local level, mechanisms such as cooperatives, community shares, or crowdfunding work well. Other ways to build trust include membership models, celebrity affiliation, certification, social media, blogging, or open days. Some see the blockchain technology as an interesting way for social enterprises to increase the transparency of their organization.

Too few energy-generating assets such as wind or solar parks have been organized and financed by the local community. Cooperatives and initiatives have started to set up collective ownership schemes to capture some of the profits for the local community. In Germany alone, there are more than 900 such energy cooperatives. Energiewerke Schönau is one such example. It has its origins in a civil initiative following the nuclear catastrophe in Chernobyl. The founder was awarded an Ashoka Fellowship for her work. The cooperative has more than 8,000 members, more than 200,000 clients, and annual revenues exceeding €200 million.

These are all elements which could be potentially addressed with a new organizational setup.

6.4 Decentralized autonomous organization (DAO) – a new organizational paradigm

A DAO is a new form of organizational setup. Kaal (2020) even postulates that it is starting to challenge the belief that governance necessitates agency.

It is an internet-native organization form which is owned and controlled by its members. A typical DAO has a central treasury for the funds collected and a decision-making process. Members do not need to know each other.

The first DAO was formed in 2016. Members contributed $150 million to an investment fund which should invest in companies and early-stage projects. However, hackers were successful in stealing roughly a third of the funds. The funds were only restored after implementing a hard fork which resulted in two separate Ethereum blockchains.

Over time, many DAOs have been formed. Many can be found in the area of decentralized finance and the area of non-fungible tokens (NFTs). However, there are also examples which are built around certain development groups or communities.

The ConstitutionDAO is an interesting example. They have collected $47 million to buy one of the original copies of the United States Constitution at an auction. After they have failed to buy the copy, the money was returned to the members. Discussions on what should be done with the copy were held online, and members voted on their preferred options.

Other recent examples of DAOs include actions to buy a copy of "Dune", a golf course, a team playing in the National Basketball Association (NBA), or land purchases in Wyoming (Chayka 2022). Another example is KlimaDAO which issues KLIMA tokens which are backed by carbon assets. A DAO is organized by a series of scripts, and creators have to decide on a number of design questions. For example, how much of the discussions should be held in public or in private forums.

Big Green is a nongovernment organization (NGO) based in Colorado which aims to connect children to healthy food with learning gardens and food literacy programs. Across the United States, they run more than 600 learning gardens and have enrolled more than 330,000 children. In 2021, the organization introduced the Big Green DAO. It is an interesting concept which allows it to experiment with new approaches in philanthropy and giving.

It was launched in November 2021, and it is likely that the governance structure will change over time. The DAO follows a few core ideas.

Each beneficiary organization of the program receives a governance token to decide on the future grantees. This is an interesting feature and is aimed at sharing

TABLE 6.3 Governance model for the Big Green DAO

DAO Committee	DAO Community
• Big Green plus 2–5 Big Green-appointed organizations. • Keyholders of multi-sig wallet. • ERC20 ExecToken for voting transparency on Snapshot platform. Tokens are nontransferable. • 1 ExecToken = 1 voting weight.	• Membership limited to grantees and donors • ERC20 GovToken for voting on Snapshot platform. Tokens are nontransferable. • Organizations reapplying for grants relinquish/burn GovToken. • Mixed-methods voting strategy for selecting organizations, allocating funds, and governance decisions.

Source: Big Green (2021).

decision-making powers with the organizations implementing the activities and which know the challenges best.

Funders will receive tokens to participate in voting. There will be a ranked choice voting to select the grantees for funding. Quadratic voting procedures will be used to vote on the funding for each selected organization. These voting procedures are rarely used and illustrate the rich design space.

Over time, the approach and structure will be progressively decentralized. One of the key ideas of this space is that power should be distributed evenly and widely.

However, there is also the tendency that a core team needs to take the first steps, and decision-making authority is spread over time.

The Big Green DAO has two governing bodies with different responsibilities shown in the table above.

There is already a large ecosystem offering DAO services such as token services, governance, treasury management, user onboarding, membership management, or security audits.

6.5 The use of the blockchain technology in the supply chain

The coronavirus pandemic has shown how much modern production relies on the international supply chain. Ports were clogged, transport prices soared, and shipping containers were missing. Cacao beans are harvested in Western Africa, and there are many reports on child labor and abuses. Smartphones depend on rare minerals sourced in the Democratic Republic of Congo under uncertain circumstances.

Coppi (2021) points out that the mapping and documenting of supply chains is the easiest part. Human rights violations happen in the areas which are not covered by the official supply chain such as work which is outsourced to families living near textile factories.

Human rights violations are often found to be related to supply chains. They usually do not happen in factories but hidden from the view of the buyers of the products or materials. Jensen, Hedman, and Henningsson (2019) find four main causes faced by the global supply chain. There is still a need for paper documents as stipulated by regulations. In addition, there is almost no standardization of information and documents. Moreover, the information in these documents needs to be updated continuously and by multiple parties. To make it even more complex, organizations usually have their proprietary information technology (IT) systems.

It can even be said that corporate profits sometimes depend on human rights violations. There is no interest to make all transactions in the supply chain transparent (Scheck and Spiess-Knafl 2020).

It is not always easy to track the supply chain. The Working Capital Fund is funding different companies which all try to improve the supply chain. For example, Phylagen is a company which uses microbiomes to identify the origins of materials.[2]

The blockchain technology is a common topic in the supply chain. The company Provenance is offering something similar. They collect data and store it in a publicly available blockchain. They describe it in the following way:

- *A brand provides their license number to Provenance, e.g., "I have a Soil Association Organic certification and have license number P1234"*
- *We pass the license number to a contract – a piece of code that runs publicly on the blockchain – to validate the brand's certificate*
- *Our contract calls the Soil Association's license checker (using a tool called Oraclize) and retrieves the renewal date for that licensee's certificate*
- *If the certificate is valid, we store the brand's identity and the renewal date along with the blockchain record for the Soil Association Organic certification mark*

The implementation using blockchain creates additional complexity and an additional layer. However, it is the only way to ensure trust in the data and the system.

Another example is "Made with Black Culture" which aims to protect the intellectual property of black artists and creators. It aims to ensure ethical commercial use of their creative energy and products.[3]

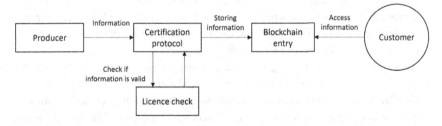

FIGURE 6.1 Structure of the model implemented by Provenance

Source: Own illustration

6.6 The use of the blockchain technology to document violence and war crimes

Starting with the Nuremberg processes, war crimes have been prosecuted in international courts. One of the challenges in conducting the trials is the quality of the evidence. Images and videos might not be valid for legal purposes. The location or the date might be missing, and there might be no proof that the evidence has not been changed. There are many archives and organizations which store the data and put the fingerprint of the image on a blockchain. The Syrian Archive has over 3 million records archived and verified more than 8,000 videos. To preserve the records, they are hashed with both md5 and sha256 and time-stamped.[4]

Arweave is a blockchain-based protocol which enables users to store data permanently. In the war between Russia and Ukraine, they have offered grants for organizations which are storing data regarding movements of troops and potential war crimes.

A problem of victims of domestic violence is the documentation of their injuries. They might not be able to go to a hospital or a police station soon after being exposed to domestic violence. Users can upload images, audio recordings, or videos to a digital safe run by HeHop. All files are signed with a private key and time-stamped. In addition, the Global Positioning System (GPS) data of the recording are added. This is a legally valid document in case it is needed for a judicial file.[5]

6.7 The use of the blockchain technology for philanthropy

Philanthropy is often considered to be a major area for the development of blockchain applications. Currently, the main ideas focus on the funding with cryptocurrencies. There is a lot of liquidity and wealth created which is addressable for philanthropic purposes.

The examples in this section do not have big traction, and it seems unlikely that all of them will be present in a few years. However, they illustrate the potential of the blockchain technology in this area.

Pawthereum is a charity project which contributes a percentage of all transactions to animal shelters across the world. It launched in late 2021 and has a market cap of around $5 million. The idea is that the token will be used by other projects, and the use of the token will contribute to its funding pot.[6]

Once the philanthropic organization is starting to implement the projects, the progress and the use of the capital can be tracked. An example for impact tracking is GiveTrack where Individuals can donate to a number of projects such as summer camps, fresh water provision, or coding schools for Black girls.[7] This is quite similar to other crowd-giving platforms. However, there is the added tracking which increases the transparency and accountability of the system.

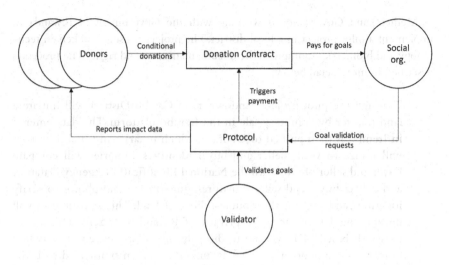

FIGURE 6.2 Structure of the model used by Alice

Source: Own illustration

Proof of impact is trying to build an infrastructure which combines the funding of interventions as well as the verification and analysis of social actions.[8] The impact space is tied to the provision of services and donors provide funds to a charity and want to track what is happening. For example, they want to know how many vaccines they have administered or how many books they have provided to young children.

The London-based organization Alice is providing a solution for this problem.[9] Donors provide funding to the organization to fulfill certain criteria and payments to the organization are only triggered when an independent expert validates the goal. This approach is very transparent, but there are also downsides. For example, it is relatively costly to have external experts validating the goals of the organization.

6.8   The documentation of land rights with the blockchain technology

Property rights are one of the most important assets, and they are a regular source of avoidable conflicts. In industrial countries, they are usually well defined and managed by a central authority. However, across large swathes of the globes, they are not well defined.

The blockchain technology offers an opportunity to record entries and transactions. Burzykowska (2021) discusses the potential for blockchain-based land registries and options for natural resources management. Many prerequisites need to be in place such as digital identities, accurate data, digital banking, as well as the ability to deliver information services to set up blockchain-based land registries.

Medici Land Governance is working with the Government of Rwanda to implement a pilot project in a local district. The project is using blockchain technology and biometrics to improve the documentation of land rights. The process is described in more detail below:[10]

> Through the pilot project, landowners in Gasabo District will initiate a land transfer by voluntary sale in the Irembo platform. The data entered in Irembo is then pushed to Ubutaka, which notaries in Gasabo District will utilize to verify seller and buyer identities. Notaries will compare buyer and seller photos with the National Identification Agency Database and collect buyer and seller signatures, fingerprints, and photos to verify identities and prevent the double-selling of land. This information will be encrypted to protect the privacy of Rwandan citizens. The notary uses web-based PKI software to digitally sign all associated identity and purchase documents, and those documents are then transferred to LAIS, where the registrar reviews, approves and signs using PKI. Upon final approval, the digital proofs of all transaction data, authorization by the notary, and approval by the registrar, are published to a public blockchain for future auditing purposes and irrefutable proof of transfer by all parties involved.

Many countries have a more informal system. For example, in Afghanistan, 80% of properties in cities are not registered and new approaches need to be tested. The UN Human Settlements Programme (UN-Habitat) has set up a system where deeds are hashed and stored on a public blockchain. Citizens can then use the system to verify the authenticity of property rights.[11]

6.9 New juridical approaches based on the blockchain technology

There is an ongoing discussion about how the persons writing the laws influence the distribution of wealth in society. Pistor (2019) highlights the role of lawyers and points toward the increasing role of programmers. Programmers are taking many design decisions when they are writing programs.

The question remains if there is even a need for some juridical systems in a blockchain-based model as they are built on the trustless mechanisms of the blockchain technology. Contracts are clear, and in theory, there is no need for courts to rule out aspects. Smart contracts can only execute what is clearly defined in their code. They have no flexibility for judgment which is necessary for most of the human interactions. However, there are instances where not every scenario can be clearly outlined.

Solving disputes between parties in different countries is usually a costly and lengthy process. Just imagine that you are based in Canada and asked a freelancer in Vietnam to deliver design services. In case that you are unsatisfied with the final result, it might be tricky to offer a good settlement procedure.

Ast and Deffains (2021) outline the early history of the online dispute resolutions industry and find the first examples in the 1990s with companies like iCourthouse. eBay tried a crowd-based model to resolve user disputes. One of the key challenges was that rulings were hard to enforce in private settings. Public courts can use the police to enforce rules. Obviously, this is not available to private resolution providers.

Courts have the role of reaching just verdicts, acquitting the innocent and sentencing the guilty. However, employing courts is a costly and lengthy process. It is unlikely that business-related cases are closed in a matter of weeks, and it usually takes months until final verdicts are reached.

Hadfield and Weingast (2013) pose the question how a legal system should be set up and what is necessary for it to function. They define courts as a classification system which can be any entity. The classification system needs to be public, noncontradictory, general, neutral, and follow an open process, among others. The classification system then produces labels such as lawful/unlawful or punishable/not punishable. This already points to a link with computer sciences.

There are already a few examples providing blockchain-based services such as Jur or Kleros (Palombo and Battaglini 2021). The White Paper describing Kleros was published in September 2019. In 2020, they won the Blockchains for Social Good Prize from the European Union's Horizon 2020 research and innovation program. The development of the protocol is managed by a French cooperative.

Kleros has developed an ingenious solution to deliver high-quality and low-cost justice settlements.[12] Two parties bring their case to Kleros and present the facts. This information is provided to an arbitration protocol which passes a judgment, and the verdict triggers the payment.

The arbitration protocol works in the following way. Jurors have to pay a fee and must forfeit it if they are not part of the majority opinion. This ensures that they are working diligently and give their best possible judgment. The fees are paid in a cryptocurrency used within the ecosystem of Kleros.

The complete code is available online and can be checked and verified by anyone.

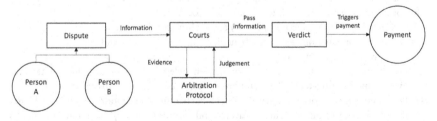

FIGURE 6.3 Structure of the model used by Kleros

Source: Own illustration

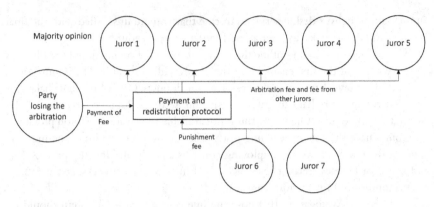

FIGURE 6.4 Arbitration protocol on the Kleros platform

Source: Own illustration

As of March 2022, they have paid 361 Ether to the jurors, of which they have 761 active jurors and resolved 1,154 disputes. The market cap of the coin is as of March 2022 around €40 million.

One of the interesting concepts of the blockchain space is how business models can be connected to each other. For example, other protocols can integrate the services of Kleros in their own processes. Marketplace can implement a dispute resolution layer in the process for those users who are not satisfied with the product.

Notes

1 There are various sources to identify and search interesting blockchain projects. See for more examples https://blockchain4sdg.com/ or http://newamerica.org/digital-impact-governance-inititiative/blockchain-trust-accelerator/reports/blockchain-impact-ledger/
2 For more information, see https://phylagen.com/
3 For more information, see https://madewithblackculture.com
4 For more information, see https://syrianarchive.org/en/data-archive
5 For more information, see https://hehop.org/en/home-en/
6 For more information, see https://pawthereum.com/
7 For more information, see www.givetrack.org/about
8 For more information, see https://proofofimpact.com
9 GitHub (https://github.com/alice-si/) and website https://alice.si/
10 For more information, see https://mediciland.com/1582-2/ and https://mediciland.com/projects/kigali-rwanda/
11 For more information, see www.un.org/en/delegate/oict-supports-un-habitat-improve-urban-planning-technology and https://unite.un.org/goLandRegistry/home
12 For more information, see www.ngi.eu/blockchainsforsocialgood/2019/12/20/kleros-the-blockchain-dispute-resolution-layer/ and https://kleros.io/en/about, https://kleros.io/en/book

7

BLOCKCHAIN AND IMPACT FINANCE

7.1 Introduction

Finance is always meant to support objectives in the public interest. Capital markets help to allocate resources to those projects, ideas, and companies with the highest value for society (Shiller 2013). In general, everything can be structured and sold on the market. It is possible to sell future music royalty payments. It is even possible to link bond payments to Ebola outbreaks as in the case of Ebola bonds. It is also possible to receive payments if there is not enough rain in a certain area. This would be the case of futures and options linked to rainfalls.

The social finance area has been innovative in adopting new models to fund social impact. The blockchain technology can be used to improve transparency and account-ability. It can also be used to record transactions and structure financial agreements as seen in the emerging decentralized finance (DeFi) space. In general, financial applications are also seen as a promising way to create social value (Venegas 2021).

It is interesting to note how the ideas about the use of the the blockchain tech-nology change over time. For example, it was a widely accepted idea that Bitcoin can be used to lower the operation costs and even reach the homeless community (Brito and Castillo 2016). For charities, there is always the risk related to the vola-tility of the cryptocurrencies. It is impossible to make meaningful budgets when the value of underlying cryptocurrency might be 50% lower or 20% higher next week or next month.

It was also widely assumed that the blockchain technology will help to disrupt the remittances industry. The blockchain technology was seen as interesting for the social impact space as it can help to lower the transaction costs. However, it is still unlikely to alleviate global poverty.

It is helpful to understand the current model used in the social finance industry. Investment funds follow a relatively expensive playbook as they charge a 2%

DOI: 10.4324/9781003218913-7

management fee and a 20% share of all profits above a certain threshold. In addition, funds can charge transaction fees, monitoring fees, or portfolio fees.

First-time fund can typically raise between 5 and 20 million. These amounts can be increased for fund managers with a longer track record. These rather small amounts make it difficult to have a sustainable business model. Fund managers can typically charge a 2% management fee. This means that the fund manager has 200,000–400,000 per year to cover all their expenses.

Funds in the impact industry also have considerably lower fund sizes than those in the traditional venture capital or private equity industry.

However, costs are usually tied to the number of transactions and not the investment amount. It is necessary to do the same analyses and due diligence checks for companies valued at €5 or €50 million. Overall, the numbers for the sustainability of funds depend thus on the fund model, regulatory requirements, as well as the business model.

Some of the innovation in the fund management industry is related to the requirements to develop a sustainable business model. For example, co-investment funds can outsource some of the due diligence activities to the partners they are working with. Some crowdfunding platforms are setting up separate funds to take advantage of the work they need to do to take funds on their platforms.

These requirements explain the attractiveness of the DeFi field for impact investors.

For all investment structures, there remains the need to generate financial returns. This might lead to the exclusion of certain target groups. For example, funds are usually not targeting the bottom of the pyramid but rather those in the middle of the pyramid. If investors want to target refugees, it is hard to develop business models and there might be a preference toward grants-based models.

One of the recurring themes is conflicts which are arising as part of the financing structure. The following figure shows how investment structures need to be set up. Intermediaries need to select their target group first. In case, if they consider community-based social enterprises, it is almost impossible to do equity investments as the resulting business model would not be sustainable. The same applies for social tech. It might not be possible to use debt capital, as the future cash flows are too unstable and risky.

There are many potential conflicts. Trade-off conflicts arise when capital providers have different pro-social preferences. For example, on a company level, it might be the case that a social enterprise receives capital from an equity investor and a foundation. In principle, the foundation is subsidizing the return of the equity investor, and this might lead to conflicts. There are also sustainability conflicts. It might be troubling if stakeholders have the impression that an organization is sustainable and might reduce their support (Achleitner, Spiess-Knafl, and Volk 2014).

Crowding out arises when an organization receives capital from public authorities and the public via donations. Donors might have the impression that they are already funding the organization with their taxes and start to reduce their donations (Abrams and Schitz 1978). This has a negative effect on the overall financial position

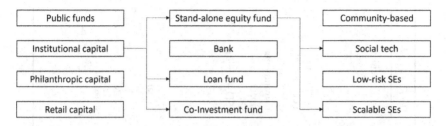

FIGURE 7.1 Illustrative structures in the financing field and the need for alignment

Source: Own illustration

of the organization. Andreoni and Payne (2011) find that this effect is mainly due to reduced fundraising activities. This leads some public authorities to ask for matching funds whereby they only provide capital when private donors contribute the same amount. There are also cases where certain income streams are incompatible. For example, schools are often prohibited from asking for additional payments from parents.

The Dubai-based private equity fund Abraaj is a good example to illustrate what can go wrong in the private equity industry and what explains the attractiveness of the blockchain technology. Abraaj was an investment fund with a focus on emerging markets such as Pakistan, Turkey, or Nigeria. However, the chief executive of the fund was found to use the funds for other purposes than investing in companies (Clark and Louch 2021). This is a problem of centralized decision-making and low transparency for outside investors. Decentralized platforms are driven by transparency and easier verification of where funds are used. This would not have been possible with the use of DeFi tools.

The following table shows typical investment funds in this area. They invest in different jurisdictions and different fields.

7.2 Investment models

There are two different models which can only be found in the field of impact finance. The first category of models is those which can be called catalytic capital, and the second category includes the pay for success models.

Catalytic capital can be defined as "debt, equity, guarantees, and other investments that accept disproportionate risk and/or concessionary returns relative to a conventional investment in order to generate positive impact and enable third-party investment that otherwise would not be possible."[1]

These are mostly investments that generate positive financial returns and impacts but are also attracting third-party capital. The first type of catalytic capital improves the capital structure so that the enterprise can take on additional capital through an improved capital ratio. Bankers speak of additional firepower as it is measured as Net Debt/EBITDA. Cooperatives are often following such a model. Energy

TABLE 7.1 Examples of funds in the impact investing space

Fund	Acumen	Capria Network	LGT Venture Philanthropy	Village Capital	The Rise Fund
Headquarters	New York	Seattle	Zurich	Washington, D.C.	San Francisco
Year of foundation	2001	2015 (accelerator program)	2007	2009	2016
Description based on the mission statement	Collecting donations to invest in companies	Network of 19 collaborating fund managers in emerging markets	Using grants and investments to support enterprises globally	Business angel investor in early-stage start-ups based on peer selection	Investments in companies with measurable environmental impact
Assets under management	USD 126 million	USD 350 million[a]	Not publicly available (n/a)	>USD 18 million	USD 4 billion
Number of investments	126	157	51	110	25
Geographical focus	Globally (64% in East Africa, India, Pakistan)	25 countries	Global	Global	Global
Fields	Agriculture, clean energy, education, and healthcare	Across all sectors	Agriculture, education, employment and skills, energy, health, housing, and information and communications technology	Agriculture, health, energy, education, financial services	Across all sectors

Fund	Aavishkaar	Bamboo Capital	PG Impact Investments	Leapfrog Investments	XSML
Headquarters	Mumbai	Luxembourg	Zug, Switzerland	London	Amsterdam
Year of foundation	2001	2007	2015	2007	2008
Description based on the mission statement	Investments in early-stage companies	Investments lead growth and social impact by anticipating major market trends.	Backed by one of the largest private markets' investment managers.	Investments in high-growth, purpose-driven financial services and healthcare businesses	Investments in small- and medium-sized enterprises (SMEs)
Assets under management	USD 1 billion	USD 400 million	USD 210 million	USD 1 billion	USD 69 million
Number of investments	68 investments	46 investments	6	n/a	~50–60
Geographical focus	India, Africa, and Southeast Asia	Global	Global	Africa, Asia	Central African Republic, Democratic Republic of Congo, Republic of Congo, Uganda, and the Republic of Congo
Fields	Across all sectors	Finance, energy, and healthcare	Financial inclusion, housing, energy, agriculture, healthcare, education	Financial services, healthcare	Agribusiness, education, health, hospitality, retail, services, transport, manufacturing

a USD 100 million is in a separate Capria Fund which invests in the fund managers.

Source: Scheck and Spiess-Knafl (2020).

TABLE 7.2 Examples of alternative investment entities

Fund	Media Development Fund	Humanity United	Working Capital Fund	International Committee of the Red Cross (ICRC) Humanitarian Impact Bond	Kois Refugee Investment Impact Bond
Headquarters	New York and Prague	San Francisco and Washington D.C.	San Francisco	Geneva, Switzerland	Belgium Brussels, Belgium
Description	Investments for independent media	Foundation dedicated to cultivating the conditions for enduring freedom and peace	Solutions to protect and empower vulnerable workers in global supply chains.	Providing services to person with a disability	Providing skills training and entrepreneurship support; targeted for refugees
Year of creation	1995	2011	2018	2017	2020
Assets under management	USD 111.6 million	n/a	n/a	CHF 26 million	USD 20 million
Number of investments	119 clients and 368 projects across 42 countries	n/a	8	3	2
Geographical focus	Global	Global	Global	Nigeria, Mali, and Democratic Republic of Congo	Target groups are Syrian refugees and vulnerable populations in Lebanon and Jordan
Fields	Media	Forced labor and human trafficking, peace building and conflict transformation	Supply chain solutions	People with disabilities in conflict-hit countries	Education
Financing instruments	Equity, debt, and hybrid capital	Grants	Commercial capital	Social impact bond	Social impact bond

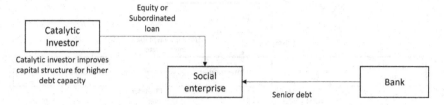

FIGURE 7.2 Improvement of the capital structure using catalytic capital

Source: Own illustration

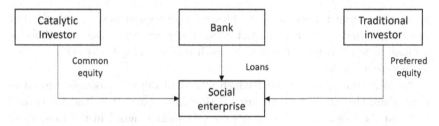

FIGURE 7.3 Catalytic capital in a deal-based structure

Source: Own illustration

cooperatives often take equity capital from their members and can use this equity capital base to fund their business.

The second type is improving the capital structure on a deal-by-deal basis. A catalytic capital provider takes on a junior position and takes a larger part of the risk. Thus, other investors can participate in the investment round and provide additional capital.

The figure above shows how different investors take on different positions which all have different levels of risk.

None of these models would be a good fit for a blockchain-based model. There are many challenges related to setting up these structures and involve contractual negotiations between the different partners.

Another category of financing instruments links the social impact to payment. These models are called "pay for success" models, and they come in all forms and shapes. All of them are built on payments which are linked to results of an intervention.

For example, the public authorities agree to pay if a certain percentage of the target group is not going back to prison. The resulting savings are then shared with the organizations implementing these interventions. Social impact bonds are the best-known model which follows a pay for success model. Thereby, a public authority enters an agreement in which it promises to pay for savings in the system.

There is a discussion about the efficiency of these models. These models add a layer of complexity and costs. In addition, public authorities usually do not need

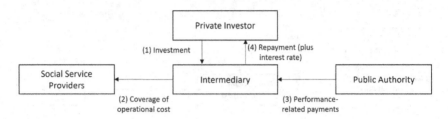

FIGURE 7.4 Structure of a social impact bond

Source: Scheck and Spiess-Knafl (2020)

prefinancing from private investors. However, participants always stress the fact that the preparation of social impact bonds brings representatives from different institutions together for conversations which they would not have without these social impact bonds.

An interesting model is Rikx which is a social impact marketplace based in Rotterdam. The city is experimenting with social impact tokens and has created Rikx. At the beginning of 2022, it won a $1 million award in the Bloomberg Philanthropies' Mayors Challenge to scale the concept.[2]

Companies with public contracts from the city have an obligation to meet certain social objectives. They can fulfill their requirements by buying tokens on the platform. It is a similar concept to the offsets in the carbon market, whereby social enterprises generate these social "offsets."

The platform is thus creating a market for social impact. The platform always has a range of investment options. One example is the Swapshop which runs a circular economy business model and guarantees to employ eight Rotterdammers for a certain period of time. She Matters is a training program which will train and prepare ten women for the job market. Mama Foundation will train ten women to become executive chauffeurs.

Pandemic and Ebola bonds are other good examples how financial instruments can be linked to certain events unrelated to balance sheets and income statements.

In 2021, Jamaica has issued a catastrophe bond where the repayment is linked to natural disaster. It will protect the country against losses from named storms for three tropical cyclone seasons until the end of 2023 (World Bank 2021).

One of the first bonds related to catastrophes was the Ebola bond. It was often criticized for late payouts, unclear terms, and high payments for the investors (Jonas 2019). These examples show that there is scope for automatic payments after certain thresholds trigger the payment.

7.3 The potential of the blockchain technology for the field

In 2019, UNICEF launched the CryptoFund. It is basically a cryptocurrency account which allows UNICEF to receive and disburse cryptocurrencies. One argument is that the publicly available records improve the accountability and the transparency of the fund and its uses. It is thus a new fundraising tool which also increases the transparency of its uses.

The CryptoFund provides details for all transactions. For example, on June 18, 2020, the CryptoFund sent 125 Ether to OS City.[3] At the time of the transaction, the Ether Price was at $231.24.

Cameroon-based Ejara is aiming to offer financial services to underserved consumers in the French-speaking countries of West Africa. It received $2 million in a recent funding round which involved Mercy Corps Ventures. The main idea is to enable the mass market to invest in cryptocurrencies, stablecoins, and tokenized assets. The blockchain technology should enable the company to lower the cost of the services and offer faster transaction speeds. For example, it also enables them to offer fractional shares to invest in.

On balance, there are surely benefits. Access to stablecoins offers protection against inflationary pressures, and alternatives to the existing banking environment are surely worthwhile to consider.

DeFi is a replication of the existing financial infrastructure in a blockchain environment. Most of the protocols are currently built on top of the Ethereum blockchain, but it is quickly changing due to high transaction costs.

The existing financial infrastructure can be characterized by a high degree of centralization. A few major intermediaries centralize functions and financial resources. It also makes sense as centralization enables scale to develop the relevant expertise and resources (Zetzsche, Arner, and Buckley 2020). London, Paris, New York, Hong Kong, or Singapore are examples for cities which are clusters for the relevant expertise. London and New York also serve as centers for legal innovation (Pistor 2019).

The OECD (2022) sees three differentiating features which define the DeFi space. The applications are noncustodial, self-governed, and community driven as well as composable. Every application is noncustodial. That means that participants control their assets with their own private keys. There are services which offer the management of private keys, but it is usually advisable for users to control their private keys.

The protocols of the applications are usually open source implying that every member of the community can review the code and check the trustworthiness. Of course, there is also the risk of hacks and flaws in the design which can lead to losses for the investors.

An intriguing element of the applications is the permissionless composability. Applications can use elements of other applications to design a new product for users.

DeFi aims to provide similar services as banks or other financial institutions in a permissionless way. That means that there is no gateway or centralized entity but only transparent and open algorithms which take decisions based on transparent rules.

The DeFi summer was in the summer of 2020 when many applications began to become popular. At the beginning of 2022, the DeFi market has a total volume measured as the total value locked of $71 billion. Roughly 50% is locked in lending protocols, 25% in decentralized exchanges, 19% in asset-based protocols, and the remaining 5% in protocols based on derivatives and payments. In total, 22% of the total assets in the DeFi space are locked in the Maker protocol.

The surprising aspect is that all transactions are conducted by algorithms, and there are no legal entity investors could sue. Given the lack of personal relationships and the total anonymity, it is obvious that most lending is based on those transactions which have some kind of collateral. In most cases, it will be one of the larger cryptocurrencies which lenders can put as a collateral. Given that there is no trust between the participants, transactions are usually asset-backed.

Conceptually, DeFi is the evolution of the P2P model (peer-to-peer) known from different platforms to a user-to-smart-contract model (OECD 2022b). This approach promises many benefits for clients. It is completely transparent and algorithmically controlled. There is little risk that managers or entrepreneurs can take the money and run. The network is also very reliable. Ethereum has been running since July 2015, and there has been no downtime since then.

There are no working hours, and transactions can be settled within minutes and not within days as it happens in public capital markets. The toolbox is very large, and financial intermediaries can offer all kinds of services. Smart contracts can be executed at the same time, thereby reducing the counterparty risk.

There are usually several core features associated with DeFi. It is open in the sense that everyone can check transactions. Just imagine that you know exactly how your bank decides on the provision of loans and how much every client is paying annually. It is permissionless in the sense that no one can restrict individuals to participate in a protocol. It is modular or interoperable in the sense that different protocols can interact with each other.

The aspects above are also of relevance for law-enforcement agencies and regulatory authorities. The permissionless nature of the applications means that anyone can use these platforms for financial purposes. This is often in contrast with anti-money laundering (AML) and other regulations across the world.

Stopping payments, freezing assets, or enforcing sanctions is a key tool for public authorities. Payment providers are usually required to enforce the requests which is widely seen to be important to establish the rule of law. The blockchain community was widely discussing the approach of the Canadian government to freeze the accounts of those protesting the pandemic measures. For example, a popular crowdfunding platform was deciding to stop all payments to the protesters. Other payment providers were also requested by the Canadian government to stop their payments. Public authority would have very limited options to limit the access to financial transactions when transactions take place in a blockchain environment.

Zetzsche, Arner, and Buckley (2020) see a few areas related to these issues. For example, it is almost impossible to determine which national jurisdiction should be considered. Given that there are no separate entities responsible for running a DeFi application, it is hard to imagine enforcement of rules. In addition, there are issues related to data protection and privacy.

There can be errors in the smart contracts underlying these protocols. Some protocols rely on admin keys to have access to improve and upgrade certain parts of the protocol. It makes sense to keep admin keys at the beginning as errors in the code base need to be corrected. There can also be issues related to the governance structure. In a recent example, Build Finance decentralized autonomous organization (DAO) lost all its assets as one perpetrator took over the treasury with a proposal which was passed in February 2022 (Copeland 2022).

In addition, there is a certain dependency on key infrastructure such as Oracles which provide the necessary external data for smart contracts.

The numbers which are settled and transacted in this ecosystem are quite high. The protocols run on Ethereum have already settled a few trillion dollars in transactions. Protocols running automatically have collected and gathered close to $100 billion.

In terms of structure, there is a settlement layer which is the blockchain used to store data and settle transactions. On top of the settlement layer is the asset layer. It includes the different tokens. Tokens can be relatively easily issued on top of the Ethereum blockchain. Fungible tokens on ERC 20 are usually coins such as Numeraire (NMR) or Kleros (PNK). Non-fungible tokens (NFTs) issue the tokens on ERC 271. The protocol layer is providing protocols for certain use cases such as exchange, lending, derivatives, or asset management, among others.

The application layer is built on top of the protocol layer. For example, MakerDAO has 400 apps and services which are built on top of the protocol. Pool DAI is offering to pool money together, lend it on the Maker platform, and donate the interest payment to a certain philanthropic project.[4]

The top layer which Schär (2021) calls the application layer creates user-friendly interfaces and allows individuals to access various applications at the same time.

There are three models for tokens which are off-chain collateral, on-chain collateral, and no collateral (Schär 2021). Off-chain means that there is a third party such as an escrow service which will act on the promise. Some of the larger stablecoins are backed by off-chain collaterals. On-chain collateral means that the assets are stored on the blockchain, and there is a smart contract which will unlock the assets as programmed. The third category means that there is no collateral, and it completely depends on the integrity of the counterparty.

7.4 Lending protocols

MakerDAO is a good case study to illustrate some of the potential features of new financing schemes. It is an interesting case study as they have managed to mobilize more than $16 billion in assets. It was founded in 2014 and received $54.5 million in venture capital funding.[5]

In principle, it is a lending platform. Users can decide to deposit one of the approved assets in a smart contract which they call a vault. Financial markets would

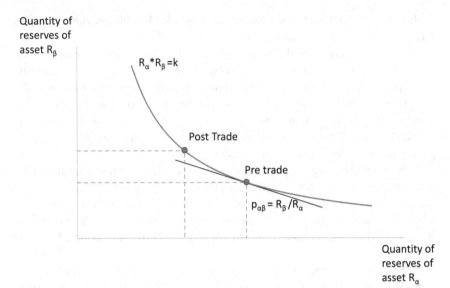

Quantity of reserves of asset R_β

$R_\alpha * R_\beta = k$

Post Trade

Pre trade

$P_{\alpha\beta} = R_\beta / R_\alpha$

Quantity of reserves of asset R_α

FIGURE 7.5 Constant product automated market marker

Source: Own illustration based on Lo and Medda (2020)

rather call it a collateralized debt position and can be compared to a bank which provides collateralized funding for real estate.

The important part is that individuals need to deposit more assets than they want to lend. This over-collateralization ranges from 101% to almost 600% on the platform. In addition, lenders have to pay a stability fee which is comparable to interest payments.

Once the user has deposited the assets, the smart contract allows the user to withdraw a US dollar-pegged stablecoin which is called DAI. That means that a user who wants to lend $1,000 in DAI needs to deposit around $1,500 in Ether in the smart contract. As of March 2022, there exist around $10 billion DAI which trade at exactly $1.00.

Users might believe in the long-term trend of the cryptocurrency and want to hold it, and in the meantime, they want to use the funds for other purposes. The table below shows a list of assets, the stability fee, and minimum collateralization ratio. RenBTC-A is a token built on the Ethereum blockchain and pegged to Bitcoin. These tokens enable owners to participate in the DeFi space.

There is a second token which is the Maker (MKR) token. There are many decisions which need to be taken. These decisions often focus on risk parameters for new assets or determine processes outside of the technical layer.

In August 2021, members voted on the budget distribution shown below. Not only the level of transparency is extraordinary but also the low costs of managing and operating the system.

TABLE 7.3 Market prices – lending

Asset	Type	Stability Fee	Minimum Collateralization Ratio
Ether	ETH-A	2.25%	145%
Ether	ETH-C	0.50%	170%
Ether	WSTETH-A	2.50%	160%
Bitcoin	WBTC-C	0.75%	175%
Bitcoin	RENBTC-A	2.50%	165%
Bitcoin	WBTC-A	3.75%	145%
Chainlink	Link-A	1.50%	165%
Yearn	YFI-A	1.00%	165%

Source: https://oasis.app/ as of March 2022.

TABLE 7.4 MakerDAO budget decisions

Core Unit	Distribution
Growth (GRO-001)	637,900 DAI
Sustainable Ecosystem Scaling (SES-001)	702,883 DAI
Content Production (MKT-001)	98,067 DAI
GovAlpha (GOV-001)	123,333 DAI
Real World Finance (RWF-001)	155,000 DAI
Risk (RISK-001)	182,000
Protocol Engineering (PE-001)	510,000 DAI
Oracles (ORA-001)	419,677 DAI
Governance Communications (COM-001)	40,500 DAI
Governance Communications (COM-001) – Continuity	121,500 DAI
Total	2,990,860 DAI

Source: MakerDAO (2021).

MakerDAO also publishes its internal budgets. For example, the Growth team has a budget of $937,950 in the stablecoin issued by the protocol. In total, 337,950 of this budget was dedicated to paying the salaries of the team members. Other items included operations, travel and partner relationships, opportunities, and integrations and marketing.

Governance token holders could also vote on the parameter changes for the assets listed on the protocol (MakerDAO 2021). The five parameter changes which were all approved by the token holders are listed below.

- The ETH-B Stability Fee will be decreased from 6% to 5%.
- The LRC-A Maximum Debt Ceiling will be decreased from 3 million DAI to 1 million DAI.
- The UNIV2ETHUSDT-A Maximum Debt Ceiling will be decreased from 10 million DAI to 0 DAI.

- The UNIV2DAIUSDT-A Maximum Debt Ceiling will be decreased from 10 million DAI to 0 DAI.
- The UNIV2DAIUSDC-A Maximum Debt Ceiling will be increased from 50 million DAI to 250 million DAI.

The level of transparency and decentralized decision-making is extraordinary and will surely be an inspiration for other developments. However, there are also risks related to this governance model. For example, there exist around 990,000 tokens, but less than 200,000 are actually locked in the governance protocol. Reasons for the low involvement are the payment of fees and the time needed to analyze the proposals. In total, 20% are thus sufficient to control the governance token.

However, token holders can designate delegates to take decisions on their behalf. As of March 2022, there are 12 recognized delegates and 11 shadow delegates. In total, they control roughly 100,000 MKR tokens. At current market prices, these tokens represent a total value of $200 million. There are a total of 990,000 tokens outstanding, and these delegates represent roughly 10% of all outstanding tokens.

The model shows how inexpensive such protocols can be run and operated. One restricting factor at the moment is the relative high gas fees which incur every time an application interacts with the blockchain.

7.5 Exchange liquidity pools or automatic market makers

One of the challenges in this field is the number of cryptocurrencies and tokens. Users might want to change their tokens such as Bitcoin into another token such as Ether. Therefore, they need exchanges which are willing to exchange or swap cryptocurrencies.

The centralized exchanges are not always the best option. Schär (2021) argues that centralized exchanges are subject to outside attacks and the little supervisory oversight might become a problem for asset owners. In effect, asset owners need to pass control of the assets to exchanges until the trade is settled. Although the risk might be temporarily limited, it is not negligible.

Decentralized exchanges provide these services with interesting protocols. Decentralized exchanges operate liquidity pools which hold a cryptoasset in each liquidity pool. Liquidity providers are incentivized to provide the liquidity of the pool and are rewarded for providing liquidity to the protocol. These exchanges work permissionless, and nobody can prohibit someone from using these services. Although they follow a relatively simple operating model, they perform well in practice (Angeris et al. 2019).

In principle, each trade changes the prices in the liquidity pool and creates arbitrage opportunities. Investors can take advantage of this arbitrage opportunity and help to move the price toward the global market price. The figure above shows the movement of prices before and after each trade. Price is thus a function of supply.

Curve is an exchange liquidity pool or automatic market maker which has only been launched in early 2020. As of March 2022, they have locked more than

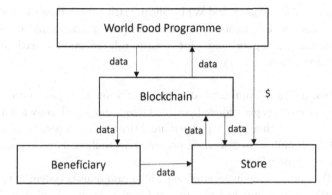

FIGURE 7.6 Structure of Building Blocks operated by the WFP

Source: Own illustration

$10 billion in the protocol and have daily volumes of $200 million.[6] Curve has launched a Curve (CRV) token which controls the Curve DAO. Token holders can decide on relevant topics such as fees, fee income distribution, or rewards for those who contribute liquidity.

Uniswap is a similar automatic market maker. Uniswap previously used the constant product function shown in the figure above but moved in March 2021 to a formula they call "concentrated liquidity." It allocates liquidity to a certain predefined price range. This is relevant for stablecoins which should always trade at a 1:1. There is no need to have a liquidity outside of these ratios.[7]

7.6 Use case in the delivery of food assistance

The World Food Programme (WFP) is delivering food assistance in 80 countries around the world.[8] The organization has set up an Innovation Lab to improve the delivery of services to those in need.

One of the problems the organization is tackling is the identification of beneficiaries in difficult environments. Imagine that you want to distribute cash or food in refugee camps or in civil war areas. For that reason, many organizations are advocating for global digital IDs which also protect privacy rights.[9] However, it remains a contested approach.

Identity tools help individuals to build a financial history or to store vaccination records or educational profiles. There are many different applications and processes, but the tool developed by the WFP shows the potential quite well. It is called Building Blocks and works in the following way:

> A Syrian woman will scan her eye to request cash back at WFP-contracted supermarkets. This will link to her account on the blockchain, and the amount of the cash distribution is automatically sent to Building Blocks. The

fact that UN Women and WFP validate each other's transaction through a common blockchain network results in improved security and accountability. There are also opportunities for cost and risk reduction, as well as increased harmonization of aid efforts.[10]

This blockchain solution has had many benefits for the organization. It reduced the dependency on paper, reduced potential fraud, and significantly reduced transaction fees. In total, they have supported more than 1 million persons every month, provided $325 million in assistance, processed 15 million transactions, and saved $2.5 million in bank fees.

WorldVision has been experimenting with a cash transfer system in rural Nepal (Coppi 2021). It was launched after the earthquake which took place in 2015.[11]

The basic idea is that any nongovernmental organization (NGO) or aid agency can disburse money to beneficiaries in remote regions. The beneficiaries do not receive cash or cryptocurrencies but rather tokens which can be used to buy goods and services in local shops. The end user only has to accept the transfer, and the more detailed paperwork has to be done by the local shop selling their goods. The transfers are stored on a blockchain which were Ethereum and Hyperledge blockchains.

During the implementation, the developers have encountered a range of obstacles (Acharya 2019). There was still a lack of adequate telecommunications infrastructure, and some users needed additional assistance to redeem their tokens. The tokens can be thought of as digital tokens which need to be redeemed in local shops. The need to establish or to partner with existing acceptance networks was an additional hurdle. Liquidity was another challenge as the local partners were hesitant to take a third-party liquidity risk. They needed to trust that the token can be exchanged for cash.

The pilot in Nepal was conducted with 105 users. The responses were positive, and costs could be substantially reduced. However, it needs to be seen how it can be implemented more widely.

There are also other approaches to facilitate payments. Nairobi-based Kotani Pay is one such example. It aims to integrate blockchain-based applications into local payment channels.[12] The problem still remains that individuals might earn cryptocurrencies but have no reliable way to exchange it in a more suitable currency for them. One of their main arguments is that gig workers might not be able to transfer their earnings back in the local currency.

In general, it is a fast-evolving space. Many concepts have vanished over the last years or completely changed their strategies.

7.7 Asset storing for refugees

Refugees usually face a long journey where they are at risk of losing their cash and other valuable items. Refugees are often subjected to exploitative practices.

Leaf offers a solution to protect their assets using blockchain technology. Users can access their fund using any mobile phone.[13] They have won awards from the United Nations, the Vatican, or the National Science Foundation.

As of March 2022, it is available for customers in Kenya, Rwanda, and Uganda. The process is relatively easy.

> Getting money into Leaf: tap on "Cash In" on the app or use the USSD menu option. Enter the mobile money number you want to request money from, including country code. Enter the amount you want to move into your Leaf Wallet. Click Submit and confirm with your PIN. Depending on your country, an SMS code may be required. The request will create a USSD popup to the person you requested money from. All they need to do is confirm with their mobile money PIN and the money will be moved instantly into your account!
>
> Getting money out of Leaf: tap on "More" and then "Cash Out" in the app or use USSD. Enter the mobile money number you want to send to, including country code. Enter the amount. Submit and confirm with your PIN. That's it! The money will be moved from your Leaf Wallet to that person's mobile money account. Remember you can cash out even across networks and borders. You can also buy airtime directly from Leaf for any phone number.

The exchange between countries is based on the open-source Stellar payment network which enables low-cost transfer across borders.

Notes

1 www.macfound.org/press/article/catalytic-capital-work/
2 For more information, see https://rikxplatform.nl/
3 For more information, see https://cryptofund.unicef.io/projects/, and for the transaction proof, see https://etherscan.io/tx/0x7df0ef84451e66e26046bb896c9ea7d4ab589b97c3fa80c080d18d0b3e22be1b
4 For more information, see https://zeframlou.github.io/pooldai/
5 For more information, see https://makerdao.com/en/
6 For more information, see https://curve.fi/
7 For more information, see https://uniswap.org/
8 The information is based on World Food Programme (2022) and Seyedsayamdost and Vanderwal (2020)
9 For example, ID2020 is advocating globally. See for more information https://id2020.org/digital-identity
10 www.unwomen.org/en/news/stories/2018/9/press-release-un-women-and-wfp-harness-innovation-for-economic-empowerment-in-crisis
11 For more information, see https://sikka.wvnepal.org/
12 For more information, see https://kotanipay.com/
13 For more information, see www.leafglobalfintech.com/

8

OUTLOOK AND FUTURE DEVELOPMENTS

8.1   Introduction

This book has shown the range of opportunities for new business models and financing mechanisms based on artificial intelligence (AI) and the blockchain technology. It has also shown the limits due to a lack of high-quality data, incomplete contracts, or a narrow scope of activities.

The recent invasion of Russia in Ukraine is a good example to see what was already used and how it was perceived in the general discussion.

On February 26, 2022, the Ukrainian government published on their Twitter feed that they are now accepting cryptocurrency donations.

> *Stand with the people of Ukraine. Now accepting cryptocurrency donations. Bitcoin, Ethereum and USDT.*
> *BTC – 357a3So9CbsNfBBgFYACGvxxS6tMaDoa1P*
> *ETH and USDT (ERC-20) – 0x165CD37b4C644C2921454429E7F9358d*
> *18A45e14*

In the first three weeks since the invasion, the Ukrainian government has raised more than $60 million. On the Ethereum blockchain, more than 70,000 transactions were registered. All transactions are public, and it is possible to see which anonymous user has donated.[1] It is possibly one of the largest crowdfunding campaigns ever and showed how the blockchain technology can be used in practice.

At the same time, governments implemented sanctions against Russian oligarchs and banks. This led some to worry that Russian individuals and companies might use cryptocurrencies to undermine the sanctions. It might have been possible in certain circumstances, but the overall trading volume is still too small to keep a large economy like Russia supplied with enough foreign currencies (Gerard 2022).

DOI: 10.4324/9781003218913-8

Weapon manufacturers have long promised that future wars will be less risky for the civil society (e.g., Davis 2019). However, the civil society suffered greatly as bombs were dropped rather indiscriminately. It also appears that most intelligence was gathered by organizations such as Bellingcat which follows an "Open Source Intelligence" approach (Higgins 2021). Evidence of war crimes is recorded on the blockchains.

AI was used for machine translation and was helpful for Ukrainian refugees to make themselves understood. However, AI was also used to create deepfake videos pretending that the Ukrainian President announced the surrender to Russia (Simonite 2022).

These examples show the range of applications, challenges, and issues society has to face when trying to fulfill the promising potential of both technologies.

8.2   Combination of AI and blockchain technologies

One of the more promising areas is the combination of AI and blockchain technologies.

Some are even referring to a convergence of AI and blockchain technologies. In general, one could say that AI is a very centralized technology where a small team of engineers is building data pipelines and algorithms. It is usually impossible to see the data, the training algorithms, or even the results. On the other side, the blockchain technology derives most of its value through its open, transparent, and decentralized approach.

Blockchain-based models follow a deterministic approach as smart contracts only follow certain predefined steps. AI-based models follow a probabilistic approach which means that they assign probabilities to certain outcomes. There might be a 96.4% probability that a farmer in rural India might repay his loan, and the decisions are taken on this basis.

In general, there are some interesting areas where convergence between both technologies can take place.

Healthcare is one of the areas which is often cited. Patients have medical records with hundreds of images and clinical reports which they might only reluctantly share with others. It might be possible to secure the access to these data with the

TABLE 8.1 Differences between AI and blockchain technology

Aspects	AI	Blockchain
Nature	Centralized	Decentralized
Access	Closed	Open
Transparency	Black box	Transparent
Approach	Probabilistic	Deterministic

Source: Singh et al. (2020).

blockchain technology and enable only doctors and hospitals to access the data if needed. The current solutions are far away from industry-wide standards, and there are many open questions to address. For example, it is not clear who is the owner of the data and the derivative products (e.g. Singh et al. 2020).

Sandner, Gross, and Richter (2020) add the Internet of Things (IoT) to the discussion. IoT devices are used in smart homes, agriculture, buildings, machines, cars, or smart grids, and they generate large amounts of data. It is impossible to analyze these data flows without the support of AI systems. A blockchain layer could increase the data security as well as data privacy for the individuals and companies using these devices.

Some of the business cases do not sound very convincing. For example, Sandner, Gross, and Richter (2020) see street lights as potential blockchain-based entities with separate wallets. Every time someone wants to have light, the person can send a micropayment to the lamp. AI can be used to optimize maintenance schedules, lighting patterns, or revenue generation.

More interesting could be these scenarios where autonomous agents operate and negotiate with other autonomous agents. It is likely that the interaction will follow standardized smart contracts, and the blockchain layer can help to document the transactions in a paper trail.

One business model which combines AI and blockchain technology is Numerai. It is a quantitative hedge fund which invites individuals to contribute models to the overall fund management model. The analysts build AI-based models using financial data provided by the hedge fund and aim to predict the stock market. Analysts have to upload their model once a week to participate in the tournament.

The interesting aspect is that analysts have to stake capital on their models. This helps to ensure that their interests are aligned with the interests of the fund. If the model performs worse than expected, the smart contract will burn a part of the amount staked at the model. Around 3,700 models are currently submitted, and almost $80 million have been paid out. As of March 2022, the market cap for the coin amounts to €150 million.[2]

In an interesting experiment, an entrepreneur connected with YCombinator and OpenAI suggested to set up an early-stage blockchain-based fund. It started with a tweet on a Saturday morning in December 2021, and within 48 hours, it was launched with the contribution of hundreds of individuals. The community and the enthusiasm for new projects is surely unknown in other fields. It is an interesting approach as it aimed to combine AI and decentralized autonomous organizations (DAOs).[3] As of March 2022, the fund is not capitalized, but entrepreneurs are invited to present their business ideas.

8.3 Criminal business models

Both technologies have also enabled new criminal business models which are often ignored. The origins of the blockchain technology are closely related to illicit activities. For example, all transactions on Silk Road had to be conducted with Bitcoin.

Silk Road was an online black market and one of the first darknet platforms.[4] Some estimates put the amount of Silk Road-related trades between 4.5% and 9% (Christin 2013).

Over time, there have been many thefts or fraudulent business models. More than 980,000 Bitcoins have been stolen from exchanges. A widely discussed case includes the Japanese exchange Mt. Gox which had lost 750,000 of client's Bitcoins (Harney and Stecklow 2017). The cryptocurrency OneCoin raised billions of dollars until its founder suddenly disappeared (BBC 2019). Ransomware victims often need to make payments in cryptocurrencies to fulfill the conditions of the attackers.

AI can be used for a number of different crimes. It involves audio and video impersonation which are often called deepfakes. It can also include the use of AI to create fake news. These fake articles can be used to influence stock market prices or even national elections. Other forms can include the use of driverless vehicles as weapons or tailored phishing (Caldwell et al. 2020).

There are many types of crimes such as white-collar crime, violent affective crime, and organized crime. Becker (1968) has introduced a stream of economic theory which explains the rationale behind criminal activity. If the utility of a crime is higher than the costs related to detection and imprisonment, then the person is likely to commit this crime.

Organized crime groups are interesting to study as they often follow entrepreneurial strategies, use institutional loopholes, react to price signals, or manage organizations often across borders. For example, sea pirates create organizations, use international legal loopholes to avoid seizure or prosecution, and change their monetization strategy according to circumstances (Boot 2009). Product pirates create unauthorized copies of successful products and thus react to market trends and forces (De Castro, Balkin, and Shepherd 2008).

The same thinking can be applied to car theft, narcotics trade, or tax fraud. All the evidence is pointing in the direction that criminals are often acting as entrepreneurs. There are many entrepreneurs such as political entrepreneurs, nonprofit entrepreneurs (Glaeser and Shleifer 2001), cultural entrepreneurs, migrant entrepreneurs, and high-impact entrepreneurs (Acs 2010), and there is some evidence to see criminals as well as entrepreneurs (Baumol 1996; Smith 1980).

Entrepreneurs use the fact that innovations per se have no orientation and can be used in any context. For example, biotechnological innovations without any inherent danger can be co-opted by persons with malicious intentions to cause harm.

There are different innovations where a criminal application is as well feasible. Just consider filesharing where legal and criminal ventures are competing for the same clients. Medical innovation is relevant for legitimate health issues but also for doping. Logistical innovations can be applied in the for-profit market as well as in the criminal market.

There are also innovations which change between social innovation and criminal innovations. Many versions of mobile banking have a social background, while the same tools are used for criminal activities. Animal protection can be used for its real purpose and for smuggling drugs across borders.

Smith (1980) makes the point that loan-sharking has a relationship with banking or that narcotics importation and wholesale trade must have something in common. Baumol (1996) argues that the pool of entrepreneurs is constant and entrepreneurs are only choosing different directions and occupations. Those occupations are either productive, unproductive, or even destructive. The choice depends on the relative payoffs the society can offer. A similar argument is used by Glaeser and Shleifer (2001) for the nonprofit sector.

There is a clear understanding that innovations are used differently across the sectors. Although the argument is rather based on the traditional for-profit sectors, Malerba (2002) sees mechanisms for different sectors at work. This is due to basic elements such as products, firms and non-firm organizations (e.g., universities or governmental authorities), sector-specific institutions, knowledge base, or technologies which interact and shape the development of the sector and its innovations. Malerba (2002) claims that these processes are sector specific.

It is also worth noting that criminal entrepreneurs are migrating between the sectors. Webb et al. (2009) note that the growth of a venture in the informal economy increases its detection risk which may result in a transition to the formal economy. This understanding is illustrated in the following figures. Each sector has its own financing and organizational structures which are determined by the constraints.

It is interesting to note that there is no criminal investment market which can be seen for social enterprises and for-profit enterprises. As Europol (2013) finds that "OCGs have limited or short resources because they rely on their criminal income for subsistence and have to reinvest a part of these criminal profits in new criminal activities."

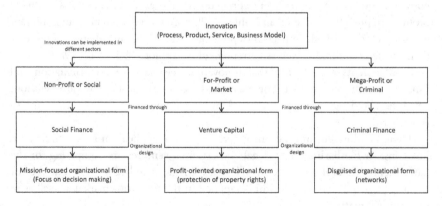

FIGURE 8.1 Sector model

Source: Own illustration

In principle, it is not possible to finance criminal entrepreneurs for a number of reasons which can be derived from the agency theory (Jensen and Meckling 1976). Capital providers need to monitor the activities of their investees. It might not be possible or they might lack the competencies. The only exceptions are organized crime groups which finance Russian hackers. Entrepreneurs need to signal to the capital provider that they are using the capital for the agreed purposes. That might not be feasible due to legal concerns.

In addition, there might be a residual loss as capital providers and entrepreneurs might not share the same goals. For these reasons, it is unlikely that criminal entrepreneurs receive external funding.

8.4   Outlook

This book focused on AI and blockchain technologies. Both technologies offer equally exciting opportunities for entrepreneurs building new marketplaces and applications. In the coming years, more user-friendly interfaces and improved usability will enable the adaptation at scale.

Both technologies face the challenge of creating networks to reach the necessary scale. AI-based business models need large datasets and blockchain-based models need a certain number of users to run a sustainable business model. A cryptocurrency is valuable only when enough users accept it for payment. However, some concepts such as non-fungible tokens (NFTs) only need a limited amount of members to function.

However, it should not be forgotten that impact is also created with social infrastructure, primary health-care services, or classroom-based education. In addition, the best models have little value if the target group is not actively involved in the model. There are many examples where projects were trying to get garbage collectors to use the blockchain technology with little additional value. It also made little sense to put bananas in Southeast Asia on the blockchain.

There are still many regulatory hurdles which are quite different across the world. While some countries embrace the technology, some regions like the European Union highlight the privacy aspects for the users (Paladini, Yerushalmi, and Castellucci 2021). Entrepreneurs regularly complain about the legal hurdles they face when rolling out their services.

The Securities and Exchange Commission (SEC) Commissioner Peirce (2020) clearly outlined the problem for the crypto entrepreneurs in a speech:

> Many crypto entrepreneurs are seeking to build decentralized networks in which a token serves as a means of exchange on, or provides access to a function of the network. In the course of building out the network, they need to get the tokens into the hands of other people. But these efforts can be stymied by concerns that such efforts may fall within the ambit of federal securities laws. The fear of running afoul of the securities laws is real. Given the SEC's enforcement activity in this area, these fears are not unfounded.

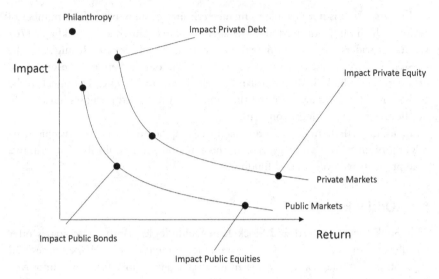

FIGURE 8.2 Trade-off between impact and return

Source: Own illustration

This quote also highlights that the decentralization is a long-term process which also needs to be managed. In addition, there is a limited understanding of how to value crypto start-ups and especially those projects which try to create impact.

This chapter has shown the building blocks and potential of decentralized finance and the potential use cases for social impact. There are currently no projects working on these solutions, and it could be an interesting opportunity.

A social decentralized finance protocol would fund impact-oriented projects and link the social impact to the payment of interest or dividends. Capital providers could indicate their impact preferences and trade tokens which possibly accrue in value. Validators would verify the impact and ensure that the capital is used accordingly. The impact–return function above could be used to design the market structure.

Notes

1 All transactions can be seen on dedicated websites such as https://etherscan.io/address/0x165CD37b4C644C2921454429E7F9358d18A45e14
2 For more information, see https://numer.ai/
3 For more information, see www.hyperscalefund.com/
4 It was an interesting field study for economists as there were no enforcements possible on the platform, and users had to trust that the supplier will ship the products.

REFERENCES

Abduljabbar, Rusul, Hussein Dia, Sohani Liyanage, and Saeed Asadi Bagloee. 2019. "Applications of Artificial Intelligence in Transport: An Overview." *Sustainability* 11 (1): 189. https://doi.org/10.3390/su11010189

Abrams, Burton A., and Mark D. Schitz. 1978. "The 'Crowding-out' Effect of Governmental Transfers on Private Charitable Contributions." *Public Choice* 33 (1): 29–39.

Acharya, Saujanya. 2019. "Sikka: Lessons Learned and Recent Developments." *Medium* (blog). March 28, 2019. https://medium.com/@saujanyaacharya/sikka-lessons-learned-and-recent-developments-8fda5b1b83cf

Achleitner, Ann-Kristin, Peter Heister, and Wolfgang Spiess-Knafl. 2014. "What Really Matters: A Theoretical Model for the Assessment of Social Enterprise Performance." In Phillip H. Phan, Jill Kickul, Sophie Bacq, and Mattias Nordqvist (eds), *Theory and Empirical Research in Social Entrepreneurship*, Cheltenham: Edward Elgar Publishing. 154–173.

Achleitner, Ann-Kristin, Eva Lutz, Judith Mayer, and Wolfgang Spiess-Knafl. 2013. "Disentangling Gut Feeling: Assessing the Integrity of Social Entrepreneurs." *Voluntas: International Journal of Voluntary and Nonprofit Organizations* 24 (1): 93–124.

Achleitner, Ann-Kristin, Wolfgang Spiess-Knafl, and Sarah Volk. 2014. "The Financing Structure of Social Enterprises: Conflicts and Implications." *International Journal of Entrepreneurial Venturing* 6 (1): 85–99.

Acs, Zoltan J. 2010. "High-Impact Entrepreneurship." In Zoltan J. Acs, David B. Audretsch (eds) *Handbook of Entrepreneurship Research*, 165–182. Springer.

Alarie, Benjamin, Anthony Niblett, and Albert H. Yoon. 2018. "How Artificial Intelligence Will Affect the Practice of Law." *University of Toronto Law Journal* Volume 68 Issue supplement 1, January 2018, pp. 106-124 March. https://doi.org/10.3138/utlj.2017-0052

Allhutter, Doris, Florian Cech, Fabian Fischer, Gabriel Grill, and Astrid Mager. 2020. "Algorithmic Profiling of Job Seekers in Austria: How Austerity Politics Are Made Effective." *Frontiers in Big Data* 3: 5. https://doi.org/10.3389/fdata.2020.00005

Altemeyer, Boris. 2019. "Making the Business Case for AI in HR: Two Case Studies." *Strategic HR Review*. Vol. 18 No. 2, pp. 66-70. https://doi.org/10.1108/SHR-12-2018-0101

Andolfatto, David. 2018. "Blockchain: What It Is, What It Does, and Why You Probably Don't Need One." *Federal Reserve Bank of St. Louis Review* 100 (2): 87–95.

Andreoni, James, and A. Abigail Payne. 2011. "Is Crowding out Due Entirely to Fundraising? Evidence from a Panel of Charities." *Journal of Public Economics* 95 (5–6): 334–343.

Angeris, Guillermo, Hsien-Tang Kao, Rei Chiang, Charlie Noyes, and Tarun Chitra. 2019. "An Analysis of Uniswap Markets." *ArXiv Preprint ArXiv:1911.03380.*

Ankenbrand, Thomas, Denis Bieri, Roland Cortivo, Johannes Hoehener, and Thomas Hardjono. 2020. "Proposal for a Comprehensive (Crypto) Asset Taxonomy." In *2020 Crypto Valley Conference on Blockchain Technology (CVCBT)*, 16–26. https://doi.org/ 10.1109/CVCBT50464.2020.00006

Apostolakis, George, Gert van Dijk, Frido Kraanen, and Robert J. Blomme. 2018. "Examining Socially Responsible Investment Preferences: A Discrete Choice Conjoint Experiment." *Journal of Behavioral and Experimental Finance* 17: 83–96.

Arkhipov, Ilya, and Jake Rudnitsky. 2021. "In Moscow, Big Brother Is Watching and Recognizing Protesters." www.bloomberg.com/news/articles/2021-05-02/in-moscow-big-brother-is-watching-and-recognizing-protesters

Asimov, Isaac. 1942. "Runaround." *Astounding Science Fiction* 29 (1): 94–103.

Ast, Federico, and Bruno Deffains. 2021. "When Online Dispute Resolution Meets Blockchain: The Birth of Decentralized Justice." *Stanford Journal of Blockchain Law and Policy*. https://stanford-jblp.pubpub.org/pub/birth-of-decentralized-justice/release/1

Auffhammer, Maximilian. 2018. "Quantifying Economic Damages from Climate Change." *Journal of Economic Perspectives* 32 (4): 33–52.

Badelt, Christoph. 1997. "Entrepreneurship Theories of the Non-Profit Sector." *VOLUNTAS: International Journal of Voluntary and Nonprofit Organizations* 8 (2): 162–178. https://doi.org/10.1007/BF02354193

Baharmand, Hossein, Amin Maghsoudi, and Giulio Coppi. 2021. "Exploring the Application of Blockchain to Humanitarian Supply Chains: Insights from Humanitarian Supply Blockchain Pilot Project." *International Journal of Operations & Production Management* 41 (9): 1522–1543. https://doi.org/10.1108/IJOPM-12-2020-0884

Baldominos, Alejandro, Yago Saez, and Pedro Isasi. 2019. "A Survey of Handwritten Character Recognition with Mnist and Emnist." *Applied Sciences* 9 (15): 3169.

Banerjee, Abhijit V., Shawn Cole, Esther Duflo, and Leigh Linden. 2007. "Remedying Education: Evidence from Two Randomized Experiments in India." *The Quarterly Journal of Economics* 122 (3): 1235–1264.

Barker, David JP, Johan G. Eriksson, Tom Forsén, and Clive Osmond. 2005. "Infant Growth and Income 50 Years Later." *Archives of Disease in Childhood* 90 (3): 272–273.

Bauer, Johannes M. 2018. "The Internet and Income Inequality: Socio-Economic Challenges in a Hyperconnected Society." *Telecommunications Policy*, SI: Interconnecting, 42 (4): 333–343. https://doi.org/10.1016/j.telpol.2017.05.009

Baumol, William J. 1996. "Entrepreneurship: Productive, Unproductive, and Destructive." *Journal of Business Venturing* 11 (1): 3–22. https://doi.org/10.1016/0883-9026(94)00014-X

Baumol, William J., and William G. Bowen. 1968. *Performing Arts: The Economic Dilemma – A Study of Problems Common to Theater, Opera, Music and Dance.* MIT Press.

BBC. 2019. "The Missing Cryptoqueen." BBC. www.bbc.co.uk/programmes/p07nkd84/episodes/downloads

Becker, Gary S. 1968. "Crime and Punishment: An Economic Approach." *Journal of Political Economy,* 76(2) (1968): 169–217.

Becker, Randy A., and Ronald J. Shadbegian. 2008. "The Green Industry: An Examination of Environmental Products Manufacturing." *US Census Bureau Center for Economic Studies Paper No. CES-WP-08-34.*

Bedi, Jatin, and Durga Toshniwal. 2019. "Deep Learning Framework to Forecast Electricity Demand." *Applied Energy* 238 (March): 1312–1326. https://doi.org/10.1016/j.apenergy.2019.01.113

Belhadi, Amine, Sachin S. Kamble, Venkatesh Mani, Imane Benkhati, and Fatima Ezahra Touriki. 2021. "An Ensemble Machine Learning Approach for Forecasting Credit Risk of Agricultural SMEs' Investments in Agriculture 4.0 through Supply Chain Finance." *Ann Oper Res (2021)*. https://doi.org/10.1007/s10479-021-04366-9

Bender, Emily M., Timnit Gebru, Angelina McMillan-Major, and Shmargaret Shmitchell. 2021. "On the Dangers of Stochastic Parrots: Can Language Models Be Too Big?" In *Proceedings of the 2021 ACM Conference on Fairness, Accountability, and Transparency*, 610–623. FAccT '21. Association for Computing Machinery. https://doi.org/10.1145/3442188.3445922

Benos, Evangelos, Rod Garratt, and Pedro Gurrola-Perez. 2017. "The Economics of Distributed Ledger Technology for Securities Settlement." Available at SSRN 3023779.

Berg, Tobias, Valentin Burg, Ana Gombović, and Manju Puri. 2020. "On the Rise of Fintechs: Credit Scoring Using Digital Footprints." *The Review of Financial Studies* 33 (7): 2845–2897. https://doi.org/10.1093/rfs/hhz099

Berrone, Pascual, Cristina Cruz, Luis R. Gomez-Mejia, and Martin Larraza-Kintana. 2010. "Socioemotional Wealth and Corporate Responses to Institutional Pressures: Do Family-Controlled Firms Pollute Less?" *Administrative Science Quarterly* 55 (1): 82–113.

Biancone, Paolo, and Maha Radwan. 2019. "Social Finance and Financing Social Enterprises: An Islamic Finance Prospective." *European Journal of Islamic Finance*. https://doi.org/10.13135/2421-2172/3176

Big Green. 2021. "Big Green DAO | The First Non-Profit Led Philanthropic DAO." https://dao.biggreen.org/

Birhane, Abeba, Vinay Uday Prabhu, and Emmanuel Kahembwe. 2021. "Multimodal Datasets: Misogyny, Pornography, and Malignant Stereotypes." *ArXiv Preprint ArXiv:2110.01963*.

Black, Michael L. 2016. "The World Wide Web as Complex Data Set: Expanding the Digital Humanities into the Twentieth Century and beyond through Internet Research." *International Journal of Humanities and Arts Computing* 10 (1): 95–109.

Blas, Javier, and Jack Farchy. 2021. *The World for Sale: Money, Power, and the Traders Who Barter the Earth's Resources*. Oxford University Press.

Block, Joern H., Massimo G. Colombo, Douglas J. Cumming, and Silvio Vismara. 2018. "New Players in Entrepreneurial Finance and Why They Are There." *Small Business Economics* 50 (2): 239–250. https://doi.org/10.1007/s11187-016-9826-6

Blockchain.com. 2022. "Block 722648." www.blockchain.com/explorer

Boggild, Lars. 2021. "Let's Get Explicit: The Emergence of Impact-Linked Returns in the Commercial Debt Market." In Walker, T., McGaughey, J., Goubran, S., Wagdy, N. (eds) *Innovations in Social Finance* . Palgrave Macmillan, Cham. https://doi.org/10.1007/978-3-030-72535-8_7

Bommasani, Rishi, Drew A. Hudson, Ehsan Adeli, Russ Altman, Simran Arora, Sydney von Arx, Michael S. Bernstein, Jeannette Bohg, Antoine Bosselut, and Emma Brunskill. 2021. "On the Opportunities and Risks of Foundation Models." *ArXiv Preprint ArXiv:2108.07258*.

Boot, Max. 2009. "Pirates, Then and Now: How Piracy Was Defeated in the Past and Can Be Again." *Foreign Affairs*, 88 (4): 94–107.

Bornstein, Matt, Martin Casado, and Jennifer Li. 2020. "The Emerging Architectures for Modern Data Infrastructure." https://a16z.com/2020/10/15/the-emerging-architectures-for-modern-data-infrastructure/

Borzaga, Carlo, Giulia Galera, Barbara Franchini, Stefania Chiomento, Rocío Nogales, and Chiara Carini. 2020. *Social Enterprises and Their Ecosystems in Europe – Comparative Synthesis Report*. Publications Office of the European Union.

Briganti, Giovanni, and Olivier Le Moine. 2020. "Artificial Intelligence in Medicine: Today and Tomorrow." *Frontiers in Medicine* 7:(27) www.frontiersin.org/article/10.3389/fmed.2020.00027

Brito, Jerry, and Andrea Castillo. 2016. *Bitcoin: A Primer for Policymakers*. 2nd ed. Mercatus Center at George Mason University.

Brown, Jason, Joe Burke, and Ashley Sauciuc. 2021. "Workforce Diversity and Artificial Intelligence: Implications for AI Integration into Performance Evaluation Systems." Available at SSRN 3861906.

Buchanan, Ben, Andrew Lohn, Micah Musser, and Katerina Sedova. 2021. "Truth, Lies, and Automation: How Language Models Could Change Disinformation." Center for Security and Emerging Technology. https://doi.org/10.51593

Buolamwini, Joy, and Timnit Gebru. 2018. "Gender Shades: Intersectional Accuracy Disparities in Commercial Gender Classification." In *Conference on Fairness, Accountability and Transparency*, 77–91.

Burzykowska, Anna. 2021. "Blockchain, Earth Observation and Intelligent Data Systems: Implications and Opportunities for the Next Generation of Digital Services." In Benedetta Cappiello, Gherardo Carullo (eds) *Blockchain, Law and Governance*, 243–258. Springer.

Busch, Timo, Peter Bruce-Clark, Jeroen Derwall, Robert Eccles, Tessa Hebb, Andreas Hoepner, Christian Klein, et al. 2021. "Impact Investments: A Call for (Re)Orientation." *SN Business & Economics* 1 (2): 33. https://doi.org/10.1007/s43546-020-00033-6

Caldwell, M., J. T. A. Andrews, T. Tanay, and L. D. Griffin. 2020. "AI-Enabled Future Crime." *Crime Science* 9 (1): 14. https://doi.org/10.1186/s40163-020-00123-8

Chaaban, Ibrahim, and Michael R. Scheessele. 2007. "Human Performance on the USPS Database." Report, Indiana University South Bend.

Chamola, Vinay, Vikas Hassija, Vatsal Gupta, and Mohsen Guizani. 2020. "A Comprehensive Review of the COVID-19 Pandemic and the Role of IoT, Drones, AI, Blockchain, and 5G in Managing Its Impact." *IEEE Access* 8: 90225–90265.

Chayka, Kyle. 2022. "The Promise of DAOs, the Latest Craze in Crypto." *The New Yorker*, January 28, 2022. www.newyorker.com/culture/infinite-scroll/the-promise-of-daos-the-latest-craze-in-crypto

Cheah, Eng-Tuck, Dima Jamali, Johnnie EV Johnson, and Ming-Chien Sung. 2011. "Drivers of Corporate Social Responsibility Attitudes: The Demography of Socially Responsible Investors." *British Journal of Management* 22 (2): 305–323.

Cheema-Fox, Alex, Bridget R. LaPerla, Hui (Stacie) Wang, and George Serafeim. 2021. "Corporate Resilience and Response to COVID-19." *Journal of Applied Corporate Finance* 33 (2): 24–40. https://doi.org/10.1111/jacf.12457

Chen, Andrew. 2021. *The Cold Start Problem: How to Start and Scale Network Effects*. Harper Business.

Chohan, Usman W. 2021. "The Double Spending Problem and Cryptocurrencies." SSRN Scholarly Paper ID 3090174. Social Science Research Network. https://doi.org/10.2139/ssrn.3090174

Christin, Nicolas. 2013. "Traveling the Silk Road: A Measurement Analysis of a Large Anonymous Online Marketplace." In *Proceedings of the 22nd International Conference on World Wide Web*, 213–224. https://dl.acm.org/doi/10.1145/2488388.2488408

Clark, C. Rosenzweig, W. Long, D. Olsen, S. (2004): Double Bottom Line Project Report: Assessing Social Impact in Double Line Ventures, Methods Catalog, Columbia Business School

Clark, Simon, and Will Louch. 2021. *The Key Man: The True Story of How the Global Elite Was Duped by a Capitalist Fairy Tale*. Harper Business.

Coase, Ronald Harry. 1937. "The Nature of the Firm." *Economica* 4 (16): 386–405.

Copeland, Tim. 2022. "Build Finance DAO Suffers 'hostile Governance Takeover,' Loses $470,000." www.theblockcrypto.com/post/134180/build-finance-dao-suffers-hostile-governance-takeover-loses-470000

Coppi, Giulio. 2021. "Introduction to Distributed Ledger Technologies for Social, Development, and Humanitarian Impact." In Benedetta Cappiello, Gherardo Carullo (eds) *Blockchain, Law and Governance*, 231–241. Springer.

Cutler, David M., and Adriana Lleras-Muney. 2006. "Education and Health: Evaluating Theories and Evidence." National Bureau of Economic Research.

Dastile, Xolani, Turgay Celik, and Moshe Potsane. 2020. "Statistical and Machine Learning Models in Credit Scoring: A Systematic Literature Survey." *Applied Soft Computing* 91 (June): 106263. https://doi.org/10.1016/j.asoc.2020.106263

Davidson, Sinclair, Primavera De Filippi, and Jason Potts. 2016. "Disrupting Governance: The New Institutional Economics of Distributed Ledger Technology." Available at SSRN 2811995.

Davis, Zachary. 2019. "Artificial Intelligence on the Battlefield: Implications for Deterrence and Surprise." *PRISM* 8 (2): 114–131.

De Castro, Julio O., David B. Balkin, and Dean A. Shepherd. 2008. "Can Entrepreneurial Firms Benefit from Product Piracy?" *Journal of Business Venturing* 23 (1): 75–90.

De Franco, Carmine, Christophe Geissler, Vincent Margot, and Bruno Monnier. 2020. "ESG Investments: Filtering versus Machine Learning Approaches." *ArXiv Preprint ArXiv:2002.07477*.

Decuyper, Adeline, Alex Rutherford, Amit Wadhwa, Jean-Martin Bauer, Gautier Krings, Thoralf Gutierrez, Vincent D. Blondel, and Miguel A. Luengo-Oroz. 2014. "Estimating Food Consumption and Poverty Indices with Mobile Phone Data." *ArXiv Preprint ArXiv:1412.2595*.

Deeks, J. J., J. Dinnes, and H. C. Williams. 2020. "Sensitivity and Specificity of SkinVision Are Likely to Have Been Overestimated." *Journal of the European Academy of Dermatology and Venereology* 34 (10): e582–e583. https://doi.org/10.1111/jdv.16382

Dees, J. Gregory. 1998. *The Meaning of Social Entrepreneurship*. Kauffman Center for Entrepreneurial Leadership.

Deming, David J. 2017. "The Growing Importance of Social Skills in the Labor Market." *The Quarterly Journal of Economics* 132 (4): 1593–1640.

Densmore, James. 2021. *Data Pipelines Pocket Reference*. O'Reilly Media, Inc.

Deparday, V., Gevaert, C. M., Molinario, G., Soden, R., & Balog-Way, S. (2019). Machine Learning for Disaster Risk Management. World Bank. http://documents.worldbank.org/curated/en/503591547666118137/Machine-Learning-for-Disaster-Risk-Management

Dixon, Chris, and Eddy Lazzarin. 2020. "The Crypto Price-Innovation Cycle." Andreessen Horowitz. May 15, 2020. https://a16z.com/2020/05/15/the-crypto-price-innovation-cycle/

Domingos, Pedro. 2015. *The Master Algorithm: How the Quest for the Ultimate Learning Machine Will Remake Our World*. Basic Books.

El Ghoul, Sadok, Omrane Guedhami, Hakkon Kim, and Kwangwoo Park. 2018. "Corporate Environmental Responsibility and the Cost of Capital: International Evidence." *Journal of Business Ethics* 149 (2): 335–361. https://doi.org/10.1007/s10551-015-3005-6

ESCO. 2022. "ESCO Portal." https://ec.europa.eu/esco/portal/occupation

Ethereum. 2022. "Introduction to Smart Contracts." https://ethereum.org

European Union. 2013. "Regulation (EU) No 346/2013 on European Social Entrepreneurship Funds." *Official Journal of the European Union.* Vol 115, 18-38. https://eur-lex.europa.eu/legal-content/EN/TXT/HTML/?uri=CELEX:32013R0346&rid=1

Europol. 2013. "EU Serious and Organised Crime Threat Assessment (SOCTA 2013)." Europol. www.europol.europa.eu/publications-events/main-reports/eu-serious-and-organised-crime-threat-assessment-socta-2013

Fradkov, Alexander L. 2020. "Early History of Machine Learning." *IFAC-PapersOnLine* 53 (2): 1385–1390.

Freeman, Karoline, Julia Geppert, Chris Stinton, Daniel Todkill, Samantha Johnson, Aileen Clarke, and Sian Taylor-Phillips. 2021. "Use of Artificial Intelligence for Image Analysis in Breast Cancer Screening Programmes: Systematic Review of Test Accuracy." *BMJ.* 2021 Sep 1;374:n1872. doi: 10.1136/bmj.n1872 PMID: 34470740; PMCID: PMC8409323.

Friberg, Jöran. 1984. "Numbers and Measures in the Earliest Written Records." *Scientific American* 250 (2): 110–119.

Friede, Gunnar, Timo Busch, and Alexander Bassen. 2015. "ESG and Financial Performance: Aggregated Evidence from More than 2000 Empirical Studies." *Journal of Sustainable Finance & Investment* 5 (4): 210–233.

Friedman, Milton. 1970. "The Social Responsibility of Business Is to Increase Its Profits." *The New York Times Magazine*, 1970.

Galema, Rients, Robert Lensink, and Laura Spierdijk. 2011. "International Diversification and Microfinance." *Journal of International Money and Finance* 30 (3): 507–515. https://doi.org/10.1016/j.jimonfin.2011.01.009

Gentle, Paul F. 2021. "Stone Money of Yap as an Early Form of Money in the Economic Sense." Financial Markets, Institutions and Risks, 5 (2), 114–119. https://doi.org/10.21272/fmir.5(2).114-119.2021

Gerard, David. 2022. "Cryptocurrency Is No Fix for Russia's Sanctions Woes." *Foreign Policy* (blog). https://foreignpolicy.com/2022/03/03/crypto-russia-sanctions/

Geremewe, Yaregal Tilahun. 2019. "The Role of Microfinance Institution for Poverty Reduction in Ethiopia." *Journal of Economics and Sustainable Development* 10 (5): 36–44.

GIIN. 2009. "What You Need to Know about Impact Investing." The GIIN. https://thegiin.org/impact-investing/need-to-know/

Gilliland, Cora Lee. 1975. "Stone Money of Yap: A Numismatic Survey." *Smithsonian Studies in History and Technology.* 1–75. https://doi.org/10.5479/si.00810258.23.1

Github. 2019. "MNIST Image by Mbornet-Hl." https://github.com/mbornet-hl/MNIST/blob/f7ee9bc8930078a8f054118d260ebfee8248677b/IMAGES/GROUPS/mnist_v5_MNIST_00001-01000_25x40.png

Glaeser, Edward L., and Andrei Shleifer. 2001. "Not-for-Profit Entrepreneurs." *Journal of Public Economics* 81 (1): 99–115.

Government Executive. 1999. "Postal Service Tests Handwriting Recognition System." Government Executive. 1999. www.govexec.com/federal-news/1999/02/postal-service-tests-handwriting-recognition-system/1746/

Grabenwarter, Uli, and Heinrich Liechtenstein. 2011. "In Search of Gamma-an Unconventional Perspective on Impact Investing." (November 25, 2011). IESE Business School Working Paper, Available at SSRN: https://ssrn.com/abstract=2120040 or http://dx.doi.org/10.2139/ssrn.2120040

Graeber, David. 2019. *Bullshit Jobs: The Rise of Pointless Work, and What We Can Do About It.* 1st ed. Penguin.

Graesser, Jordan, Anil Cheriyadat, Ranga Raju Vatsavai, Varun Chandola, Jordan Long, and Eddie Bright. 2012. "Image Based Characterization of Formal and Informal

Neighborhoods in an Urban Landscape." *IEEE Journal of Selected Topics in Applied Earth Observations and Remote Sensing* 5 (4): 1164–1176.

Greater Manchester Combined Authority. 2022. "Research: Cost Benefit Analysis." Greater Manchester Combined Authority. www.greatermanchester-ca.gov.uk/what-we-do/research/research-cost-benefit-analysis/

Griffin, Terry W., Keith D. Harris, Jason K. Ward, Paul Goeringer, and Jessica A. Richard. 2021. "Three Digital Agriculture Problems in Cotton Solved by Distributed Ledger Technology." *Applied Economic Perspectives and Policy*, 44 (1), March 2022,pp 237–252.

Guha, Abhijit, Dhruv Grewal, Praveen K. Kopalle, Michael Haenlein, Matthew J. Schneider, Hyunseok Jung, Rida Moustafa, Dinesh R. Hegde, and Gary Hawkins. 2021. "How Artificial Intelligence Will Affect the Future of Retailing." *Journal of Retailing*, Re-Strategizing Retailing in a Technology Based Era, 97 (1): 28–41. https://doi.org/10.1016/j.jretai.2021.01.005

Guo, Eileen, and Hikmat Noori. 2021. "This Is the Real Story of the Afghan Biometric Databases Abandoned to the Taliban." Eileen Guoarchive PageHikmat Noori. www.technologyreview.com/2021/08/30/1033941/afghanistan-biometric-databases-us-military-40-data-points/

Hadfield, Gillian K., and Barry R. Weingast. 2013. "Microfoundations of the Rule of Law." *Forthcoming, Annual Review of Political Science, Stanford Law and Economics Olin Working Paper* 453: 13–15.

Haenlein, Michael, and Andreas Kaplan. 2019. "A Brief History of Artificial Intelligence: On the Past, Present, and Future of Artificial Intelligence." *California Management Review* 61 (4): 5–14. https://doi.org/10.1177/0008125619864925

Hapke, Hannes, and Catherine Nelson. 2020. *Building Machine Learning Pipelines*. O'Reilly Media.

Harji, Karim, and Edward T. Jackson. "Developmental evaluation in practice: Lessons from evaluating a market-based employment initiative." *The Rockefeller Foundation. Evaluation Office* (2016): 1–12.

Harney, Alexandra, and Steve Stecklow. 2017. "Twice Burned – How Mt. Gox's Bitcoin Customers Could Lose Again." *Reuters*. www.reuters.com/investigates/special-report/bitcoin-gox/

Hart, Oliver, and Luigi Zingales. 2017. "Companies Should Maximize Shareholder Welfare Not Market Value." *ECGI-Finance Working Paper*, no. 521.

Hassan, Abul, and Sabur Mollah. 2018. *Islamic Finance: Ethical Underpinnings, Products, and Institutions*. 1st ed. Palgrave Macmillan.

Hassani, Bertrand K. 2021. "Societal Bias Reinforcement through Machine Learning: A Credit Scoring Perspective." *AI and Ethics* 1 (3): 239–247. https://doi.org/10.1007/s43681-020-00026-z

Hawkes, Nigel. 2016. "NHS Data Sharing Deal with Google Prompts Concern." *BMJ* 353 (May): i2573. https://doi.org/10.1136/bmj.i2573

Heckman, James J., and Tim Kautz. 2012. "Hard Evidence on Soft Skills." *Labour Economics*, European Association of Labour Economists 23rd Annual Conference, Paphos, Cyprus, September 22–24, 2011, 19 (4): 451–464. https://doi.org/10.1016/j.labeco.2012.05.014

Higgins, Eliot. 2021. *We Are Bellingcat: An Intelligence Agency for the People*. Bloomsbury Publishing.

High-Level Expert Group on Artificial Intelligence, AI. 2018. "A Definition of AI: Main Capabilities and Scientific Disciplines." https://ec.europa.eu/futurium/en/system/files/ged/ai_hleg_definition_of_ai_18_december_1.pdf

Höchstädter, Anna Katharina, and Barbara Scheck. 2015. "What's in a Name: An Analysis of Impact Investing Understandings by Academics and Practitioners." *Journal of Business Ethics* 132 (2): 449–475.

Hu, Ming, and Mark Sidel. 2020. "Civil Society and COVID in China: Responses in an Authoritarian Society." *Nonprofit and Voluntary Sector Quarterly* 49 (6): 1173–1181. https://doi.org/10.1177/0899764020964596

Huang, Danny. 2021. "Environmental, Social and Governance (ESG) Activity and Firm Performance: A Review and Consolidation." *Accounting & Finance* 61 (1): 335–360.

Huang, Jon, Claire O'Neill, and Hiroko Tabuchi. 2021. "Bitcoin Uses More Electricity Than Many Countries. How Is That Possible?" *The New York Times*, September 3, 2021, sec. Climate. www.nytimes.com/interactive/2021/09/03/climate/bitcoin-carbon-footprint-electricity.html

Hughes, Arthur, Michael A. Urban, and Dariusz Wójcik. 2021. "Alternative ESG Ratings: How Technological Innovation Is Reshaping Sustainable Investment." *Sustainability* 13 (6): 3551.

Iacobucci, Gareth. 2017. "Patient Data Were Shared with Google on an 'Inappropriate Legal Basis,' Says NHS Data Guardian." *British Medical Journal* 357: j2439.

Iansiti, Marco, and Karim R. Lakhani. 2020. *Competing in the Age of AI: Strategy and Leadership When Algorithms and Networks Run the World.* Harvard Business Press.

Ilie, Codrina Maria, Maria Antonia Brovelli, and Serena Coetzee. 2019. "Monitoring SDG 9 with Global Open Data and Open Software–A Case Study from Rural Tanzania." In *ISPRS Geospatial Week 2019*, 42: 1551–1558. International Society for Photogrammetry and Remote Sensing.

ImpactAlpha. 2021. "Acumen's ALIVE Backs Chilean Edtech Company UPlanner." ImpactAlpha. https://impactalpha.com/acumens-alive-backs-chilean-edtech-company-uplanner/

Indicina. 2022. "API Platform Documentation." Indicina Technologies Limited. https://developers.indicina.co/docs

Jakobson, Lev I., Stefan Toepler, and Irina V. Mersianova. 2018. "Foundations in Russia: Evolving Approaches to Philanthropy." *American Behavioral Scientist* 62 (13): 1844–1868.

Jansen, Stephan A., Clemens Mast, and Wolfgang Spiess-Knafl. 2021. "Social Finance Investments with a Focus on Digital Social Business Models." In Thomas Walker, Jane McGaughey, Sherif Goubran, Nadra Wagdy (eds) *Innovations in Social Finance*, 235–249. Springer.

Jensen, Michael C., and William H. Meckling. 1976. "Theory of the Firm: Managerial Behavior, Agency Costs and Ownership Structure." *Journal of Financial Economics* 3 (4): 305–360.

Jensen, Thomas, Jonas Hedman, and Stefan Henningsson. 2019. "How TradeLens Delivers Business Value With Blockchain Technology." *MIS Quarterly Executive* 18 (4): 5.

João-Roland, Iraci de Souza, and Maria L. Granados. 2020. "Social Innovation Drivers in Social Enterprises: Systematic Review." *Journal of Small Business and Enterprise Development* 27 (5): 775–795. https://doi.org/10.1108/JSBED-12-2019-0396

Jonas, Olga. 2019. "Pandemic Bonds: Designed to Fail in Ebola." *Nature* 572 (7769): 285. https://doi.org/10.1038/d41586-019-02415-9

Jones, Dustin. 2021. "Facebook Apologizes After Its AI Labels Black Men As 'Primates.'" *NPR*, September 4, 2021, sec. Race. www.npr.org/2021/09/04/1034368231/facebook-apologizes-ai-labels-black-men-primates-racial-bias

Jones, Karen C., and Amanda Burns. 2021. "Unit Costs of Health and Social Care 2021." Personal Social Services Research Unit, University of Kent, Canterbury. DOI: 10.22024/UniKent/01.02.92342

Junkus, Joan C., and Thomas C. Berry. 2010. "The Demographic Profile of Socially Responsible Investors." *Managerial Finance*, Vol. 36 No. 6, pp. 474–481. https://doi.org/10.1108/03074351011042955

Kaal, Wulf A. 2020. "Blockchain Solutions for Agency Problems in Corporate Governance." In *Information for Efficient Decision Making*, 313–329. World Scientific. https://doi.org/10.1142/9789811220470_0012

Kewell, Beth, Richard Adams, and Glenn Parry. 2017. "Blockchain for Good?" *Strategic Change* 26 (5): 429–437. https://doi.org/10.1002/jsc.2143

Kiayias, Aggelos, Alexander Russell, Bernardo David, and Roman Oliynykov. 2017. "Ouroboros: A Provably Secure Proof-of-Stake Blockchain Protocol." In *Advances in Cryptology – CRYPTO 2017*, edited by Jonathan Katz and Hovav Shacham, 357–388. Lecture Notes in Computer Science. Springer International Publishing. https://doi.org/10.1007/978-3-319-63688-7_12

Krauss, Nicolas, and Ingo Walter. 2009. "Can Microfinance Reduce Portfolio Volatility?" *Economic Development and Cultural Change* 58 (1): 85–110. https://doi.org/10.1086/605206

Kremer, Michael, Conner Brannen, and Rachel Glennerster. 2013. "The Challenge of Education and Learning in the Developing World." *Science* 340 (6130): 297–300.

Kučak, Danijel, Vedran Juričić, and Goran Đambić. 2018. "Machine Learning in Education – A Survey of Current Research Trends." *Annals of DAAAM & Proceedings* 29.

Kumar, K. Ranjith, and M. Surya Kalavathi. 2018. "Artificial Intelligence Based Forecast Models for Predicting Solar Power Generation." *Materials Today: Proceedings*, International Conference on Processing of Materials, Minerals and Energy (July 29th–30th) 2016, Ongole, Andhra Pradesh, India, 5 (1, Part 1): 796–802. https://doi.org/10.1016/j.matpr.2017.11.149

Landi, Giovanni, and Mauro Sciarelli. 2018. "Towards a More Ethical Market: The Impact of ESG Rating on Corporate Financial Performance." *Social Responsibility Journal* 15 (1): 11–27. https://doi.org/10.1108/SRJ-11-2017-0254

Lawrence, Judy, Paula Blackett, and Nicholas A. Cradock-Henry. 2020. "Cascading Climate Change Impacts and Implications." *Climate Risk Management* 29 (January): 100234. https://doi.org/10.1016/j.crm.2020.100234

LeCun, Yann. 1998. "The MNIST Database of Handwritten Digits." http://yann.lecun.com/exdb/mnist/

LeCun, Yann, Corinna Cortes, and Chris Burges. 1998. "MNIST Handwritten Digit Database." http://yann.lecun.com/exdb/mnist/

Lenail, Alexander. 2022. "NN SVG." http://alexlenail.me/NN-SVG/index.html

Letts, Christine W., William Ryan, and Allen Grossman. 1997. "Virtuous Capital: What Foundations Can Learn from Venture Capitalists." *Harvard Business Review* 75: 36–50.

Lo, Yuen C., and Francesca Medda. 2020. "Uniswap and the Emergence of the Decentralized Exchange." SSRN Scholarly Paper ID 3715398. Social Science Research Network. https://doi.org/10.2139/ssrn.3715398

Luther, William J., and Alexander W. Salter. 2017. "Bitcoin and the Bailout." *The Quarterly Review of Economics and Finance* 66: 50–56.

Mair, Johanna, Ignasi Marti, and Marc J. Ventresca. 2012. "Building Inclusive Markets in Rural Bangladesh: How Intermediaries Work Institutional Voids." *Academy of Management Journal* 55 (4): 819–850.

MakerDAO. 2021. "MOMC Proposal, August Core Unit Budgets, Housekeeping – August 6, 2021." https://vote.makerdao.com/executive/template-executive-vote-momc-proposal-august-core-unit-budgets-housekeeping-august-6-2021?network=mainnet#proposal-detail

Malerba, Franco. 2002. "Sectoral Systems of Innovation and Production." *Research Policy* 31 (2): 247–264.

Manski, Sarah, and Michel Bauwens. 2020. "Reimagining New Socio-Technical Economics through the Application of Distributed Ledger Technologies." *Frontiers in Blockchain* 2: 29.

Martin, Roger L., and Sally Osberg. 2007. "Social Entrepreneurship: The Case for Definition." *Stanford Social Innovation Review, 5(2)*, 29–39. https://doi.org/10.48558/TSAV-FG11

Maskin, Eric S. 2008. "Mechanism Design: How to Implement Social Goals." *American Economic Review* 98 (3): 567–576.

McCarthy, John, Marvin L. Minsky, Nathaniel Rochester, and Claude E. Shannon. 1955. "A Proposal for the Dartmouth Summer Research Project on Artificial Intelligence, August 31, 1955." www-formal.stanford.edu/jmc/history/dartmouth/dartmouth.html

McLachlan, Jonathan, and John Gardner. 2004. "A Comparison of Socially Responsible and Conventional Investors." *Journal of Business Ethics* 52 (1): 11–25. https://doi.org/10.1023/B:BUSI.0000033104.28219.92

Metz, Cade. 2021. *Genius Makers: The Mavericks Who Brought AI to Google, Facebook, and the World.* Dutton.

Mezrich, Ben. 2019. *Bitcoin Billionaires.* Luitingh Sijthoff.

Mhlanga, David. 2020. "Industry 4.0 in Finance: The Impact of Artificial Intelligence (Ai) on Digital Financial Inclusion." *International Journal of Financial Studies* 8 (3): 45.

Minsky, Marvin, and Seymour Papert. 1969. "An Introduction to Computational Geometry." *Cambridge Tiass., HIT* 479: 480.

Mithas, Sunil, Charles F. Hofacker, Anil Bilgihan, Tarik Dogru, Vanja Bogicevic, and Ajit Sharma. 2020. "Information Technology and Baumol's Cost Disease in Healthcare Services: A Research Agenda." *Journal of Service Management* 31 (5): 911–937. https://doi.org/10.1108/JOSM-11-2019-0339

Mittelstadt, Brent Daniel, Patrick Allo, Mariarosaria Taddeo, Sandra Wachter, and Luciano Floridi. 2016. "The Ethics of Algorithms: Mapping the Debate." *Big Data & Society* 3 (2): 2053951716679679.

Mittermaier, Alexandra, Dean A. Shepherd, and Holger Patzelt. 2021. "We Cannot Direct the Wind, but We Can Adjust the Sails: Prosocial Ventures' Responses to Potential Resource Threats." *Organization Science*, April, 1–26. https://doi.org/10.1287/orsc.2021.1465

Montenegro, Claudio E., and Harry Anthony Patrinos. 2013. "Returns to Schooling around the World." *Background Paper for the World Development Report*, 8258024–719.

Morley, Jessica, Mariarosaria Taddeo, and Luciano Floridi. 2019. "Google Health and the NHS: Overcoming the Trust Deficit." *The Lancet Digital Health* 1 (8): e389. https://doi.org/10.1016/S2589-7500(19)30193-1

Murero, Monica, Salvatore Vita, Andrea Mennitto, and Giuseppe D'Ancona. 2020. "Artificial Intelligence for Severe Speech Impairment: Innovative Approaches to AAC and Communication." In *PSYCHOBIT*. Conference: Proceedings of the Second Symposium of Psychology-Based Technologies: Naples, Italy

Nakamoto, Satoshi. 2008. "Bitcoin: A Peer-to-Peer Electronic Cash System." https://bitcoin.org/bitcoin.pdf.

Narayanan, Arvind, and Jeremy Clark. 2017. "Bitcoin's Academic Pedigree: The Concept of Cryptocurrencies Is Built from Forgotten Ideas in Research Literature." *Queue* 15 (4): 20–49.

Narayanan, Arvind, and Vitaly Shmatikov. 2008. "Robust De-Anonymization of Large Sparse Datasets." In *2008 IEEE Symposium on Security and Privacy (Sp 2008)*, 111–125. https://doi.org/10.1109/SP.2008.33

Nassr, Iota Kaousar. 2021. *Understanding the Tokenisation of Assets in Financial Markets*. Going Digital Toolkit, No. 19. OECD. https://goingdigital.oecd.org/data/notes/No19_ToolkitNote_AssetTokenisation.pdf

Natarajan, Harish, Solvej Krause, and Helen Gradstein. 2017. "Distributed Ledger Technology and Blockchain." https://openknowledge.worldbank.org/handle/10986/29053 License: CC BY 3.0 IGO.

Netflix. 2021. "Netflix Research." https://research.netflix.com/research-area/machine-learning

Nixon, Ron. 2013. "Last of a Breed: Postal Workers Who Decipher Bad Addresses." *The New York Times*, May 4, 2013, sec. U.S. www.nytimes.com/2013/05/04/us/where-mail-with-illegible-addresses-goes-to-be-read.html

Nordhaus, William, and Paul Sztorc. 2013. "DICE 2013R: Introduction and User's Manual." *Yale University and the National Bureau of Economic Research, USA*.

Norman, Wayne, and Chris MacDonald. 2004. "Getting to the Bottom of 'Triple Bottom Line.'" *Business Ethics Quarterly* 14 (2): 243–262.

Nti, Isaac Kofi, Adebayo Felix Adekoya, Benjamin Asubam Weyori, and Owusu Nyarko-Boateng. 2021. "Applications of Artificial Intelligence in Engineering and Manufacturing: A Systematic Review." *Journal of Intelligent Manufacturing*. April. https://doi.org/10.1007/s10845-021-01771-6

OECD. 2019. *Artificial Intelligence in Society*. OECD Publishing. www.oecd-ilibrary.org/science-and-technology/artificial-intelligence-in-society_eedfee77-en

———. 2022a. "OECD Framework for the Classification of AI Systems: A Tool for Effective AI Policies." https://oecd.ai/en/p/classification

———. 2022b. *Why Decentralised Finance (DeFi) Matters and the Policy Implications – OECD*. OECD. www.oecd.org/finance/why-decentralised-finance-defi-matters-and-the-policy-implications.htm?utm_source=Adestra&utm_medium=email&utm_content=Read%20More&utm_campaign=Why%20Decentralised%20Finance%20%28DeFi%29%20Matters&utm_term=daf

Oliveira, Luis, Liudmila Zavolokina, Ingrid Bauer, and Gerhard Schwabe. 2018. "To Token or Not to Token: Tools for Understanding Blockchain Tokens.". In: International Conference of Information Systems (ICIS 2018), San Francisco, USA, 12 December 2018 - 16 December 2018, ICIS.

O'Neil, Cathy. 2016. *Weapons of Math Destruction: How Big Data Increases Inequality and Threatens Democracy*. Crown.

Oosthuizen, Kim, Elsamari Botha, Jeandri Robertson, and Matteo Montecchi. 2021. "Artificial Intelligence in Retail: The AI-Enabled Value Chain." *Australasian Marketing Journal* 29 (3): 264–273. https://doi.org/10.1016/j.ausmj.2020.07.007

Ostrom, Elinor. 2009. *Understanding Institutional Diversity*. Princeton University Press.

Pache, Anne-Claire, and Filipe Santos. 2013. "Inside the Hybrid Organization: Selective Coupling as a Response to Competing Institutional Logics." *Academy of Management Journal* 56 (4): 972–1001.

Paladini, Stefania, Erez Yerushalmi, and Ignazio Castellucci. 2021. "Public Governance of the Blockchain Revolution and Its Implications for Social Finance: A Comparative Analysis." In Thomas Walker, Jane McGaughey, Sherif Goubran, Nadra Wagdy (eds) *Innovations in Social Finance*, 293–318. Springer.

Palombo, Alessandro, and Raffaele Battaglini. 2021. "Justice for All: Jur's Open Layer as a Case Study, Towards a More Open and Sustainable Approach." In Benedetta Cappiello, Gherardo Carullo (eds) *Blockchain, Law and Governance*, 259–274. Springer.

Parida, Vinit, David Sjödin, and Wiebke Reim. 2019. *Reviewing Literature on Digitalization, Business Model Innovation, and Sustainable Industry: Past Achievements and Future Promises*. Multidisciplinary Digital Publishing Institute.

Park, Cyn-Young, and Rogelio Mercado Jr. 2018. "Financial Inclusion, Poverty, and Income Inequality." *The Singapore Economic Review* 63 (01): 185–206.

Peirce, Hester M. 2020. "Running on Empty: A Proposal to Fill the Gap Between Regulation and Decentralization." www.sec.gov/news/speech/peirce-remarks-blockress-2020-02-06

Perdana, Arif, Alastair Robb, Vivek Balachandran, and Fiona Rohde. 2021. "Distributed Ledger Technology: Its Evolutionary Path and the Road Ahead." *Information & Management* 58 (3): 103316. https://doi.org/10.1016/j.im.2020.103316

Phills, James A., Kriss Deiglmeier, and Dale T. Miller. 2008. "Rediscovering Social Innovation." *Stanford Social Innovation Review* 6 (4): 34–43.

Piketty, Thomas. 2018. *Capital in the Twenty-First Century.* Harvard University Press.

Pinna, Andrea, and Wiebe Ruttenberg. 2016. "Distributed Ledger Technologies in Securities Post-Trading Revolution or Evolution?" *ECB Occasional Paper*, no. 172.

Pistor, Katharina. 2019. *The Code of Capital.* Princeton University Press.

Pollack, Andrew. 1983. "Technology: The Computer as Translator." *The New York Times*, April 28, 1983, sec. Business. www.nytimes.com/1983/04/28/business/technology-the-computer-as-translator.html

Porter, Michael E., and Mark R. Kramer. 2019. "Creating Shared Value." In : Lenssen, G., Smith, N. (eds) *Managing Sustainable Business*, 323–346. Springer, Dordrecht. https://doi.org/10.1007/978-94-024-1144-7_16

Prahalad, Coimbatore Krishna, Coimbatore K. Prahalad, and Harvey C. Fruehauf. 2005. *The Fortune at the Bottom of the Pyramid.* Wharton School Pub.

Prates, Marcelo O. R., Pedro H. Avelar, and Luís C. Lamb. 2020. "Assessing Gender Bias in Machine Translation: A Case Study with Google Translate." *Neural Computing and Applications* 32 (10): 6363–6381. https://doi.org/10.1007/s00521-019-04144-6

Pschetz, Larissa, Billy Dixon, Kruakae Pothong, Arlene Bailey, Allister Glean, Luis Lourenço Soares, and Jessica A. Enright. 2020. "Designing Distributed Ledger Technologies for Social Change: The Case of CariCrop." In *Proceedings of the 2020 CHI Conference on Human Factors in Computing Systems*, 1–12. CHI '20. Association for Computing Machinery. https://doi.org/10.1145/3313831.3376364

Raghukumar, Kaustubha, Grace Chang, Frank Spada, Craig Jones, Tim Janssen, and Andrew Gans. 2019. "Performance Characteristics of 'Spotter,' a Newly Developed Real-Time Wave Measurement Buoy." *Journal of Atmospheric and Oceanic Technology* 36 (6): 1127–1141.

Rauchs, Michel, Andrew Glidden, Brian Gordon, Gina C. Pieters, Martino Recanatini, Francois Rostand, Kathryn Vagneur, and Bryan Zheng Zhang. 2018. "Distributed Ledger Technology Systems: A Conceptual Framework." Available at SSRN 3230013.

Ribeiro, I., P. Sobral, P. Peças, and E. Henriques. 2018. "A Sustainable Business Model to Fight Food Waste." *Journal of Cleaner Production* 177 (March): 262–275. https://doi.org/10.1016/j.jclepro.2017.12.200

Rolnick, David, Priya L. Donti, Lynn H. Kaack, Kelly Kochanski, Alexandre Lacoste, Kris Sankaran, Andrew Slavin Ross, Nikola Milojevic-Dupont, Natasha Jaques, and Anna Waldman-Brown. 2019. "Tackling Climate Change with Machine Learning." *ArXiv Preprint ArXiv:1906.05433.*

Ross, Greg, Sanjiv Das, Daniel Sciro, and Hussain Raza. 2021. "CapitalVX: A Machine Learning Model for Startup Selection and Exit Prediction." *The Journal of Finance and Data Science* 7 (November): 94–114. https://doi.org/10.1016/j.jfds.2021.04.001

Rubeis, Giovanni. 2020. "The Disruptive Power of Artificial Intelligence. Ethical Aspects of Gerontechnology in Elderly Care." *Archives of Gerontology and Geriatrics* 91 (November): 104186. https://doi.org/10.1016/j.archger.2020.104186

Rüede, Dominik, and Kathrin Lurtz. 2012. "Mapping the Various Meanings of Social Innovation: Towards a Differentiated Understanding of an Emerging Concept." (July 19, 2012). EBS Business School Research Paper No. 12-03 Available at SSRN: https://ssrn.com/abstract=2091039 or http://dx.doi.org/10.2139/ssrn.2091039

Russakovsky, Olga, Jia Deng, Hao Su, Jonathan Krause, Sanjeev Satheesh, Sean Ma, Zhiheng Huang, Andrej Karpathy, Aditya Khosla, and Michael Bernstein. 2015. "Imagenet Large Scale Visual Recognition Challenge." *International Journal of Computer Vision* 115 (3): 211–252.

Russell, Stuart, and Peter Norvig. 2020. *Artificial Intelligence: A Modern Approach.* 4th ed. Pearson.

Samuel, Arthur L. 1959. "Some Studies in Machine Learning Using the Game of Checkers." *IBM Journal of Research and Development* 3 (3): 210–229.

Sandner, Philipp, Jonas Gross, and Robert Richter. 2020. "Convergence of Blockchain, IoT, and AI." *Frontiers in Blockchain* 3. www.frontiersin.org/article/10.3389/fbloc.2020.522600

Santos, Filipe M. 2012. "A Positive Theory of Social Entrepreneurship." *Journal of Business Ethics* 111 (3): 335–351.

Sarma, Mandira. 2008. "Index of Financial Inclusion." Working paper.

Saygili, Ebru, Serafettin Arslan, and Ayse Ozden Birkan. 2021. "ESG Practices and Corporate Financial Performance: Evidence from Borsa Istanbul." *Borsa Istanbul Review*, July. https://doi.org/10.1016/j.bir.2021.07.001

Schär, Fabian. 2021. "Decentralized Finance: On Blockchain-and Smart Contract-Based Financial Markets." *FRB of St. Louis Review.* Vol. 103, No. 2 https://research.stlouisfed.org/publications/review/2021/02/05/decentralized-finance-on-blockchain-and-smart-contract-based-financial-markets

Scheck, Barbara, and Wolfgang Spiess-Knafl. 2020. "Impact Investing in the Framework of Business and Human Rights." European Parliament. www.europarl.europa.eu/thinktank/de/document.html?reference=EXPO_IDA(2020)603490

Schetsche, Michael. 2014. "Die Empirische Analyse Sozialer Probleme." In *Empirische Analyse Sozialer Probleme: Das Wissenssoziologische Programm*, edited by Michael Schetsche, 57–173. Fachmedien. https://doi.org/10.1007/978-3-658-02280-8_2

Serafeim, George. 2020. "Public Sentiment and the Price of Corporate Sustainability." *Financial Analysts Journal* 76 (2): 26–46.

Seyedsayamdost, Elham, and Peter Vanderwal. 2020. "From Good Governance to Governance for Good: Blockchain for Social Impact." *Journal of International Development* 32 (6): 943–960. https://doi.org/10.1002/jid.3485

Shankar, Shreya, Yoni Halpern, Eric Breck, James Atwood, Jimbo Wilson, and D. Sculley. 2017. "No Classification without Representation: Assessing Geodiversity Issues in Open Data Sets for the Developing World." *ArXiv:1711.08536*, November. http://arxiv.org/abs/1711.08536

Sharma, Meenu, Meenakshi Gupta, Roop Lal Sharma, and Ajay Kumar Sharma. 2021. "Prospects and Challenges of Microfinance as a Tool in Poverty Reduction." *Academy of Marketing Studies Journal* 25 (6): 1–6.

Shaw, Eleanor, and Sara Carter. 2007. "Social Entrepreneurship." *Journal of Small Business and Enterprise Development*, 14 (3): pp. 418–434. https://doi.org/10.1108/14626000710773529

Shiller, Robert J. 2013. *Finance and the Good Society.* Princeton University Press.

Simonite, Tom. 2022. "A Zelensky Deepfake Was Quickly Defeated. The Next One Might Not Be." *Wired.* www.wired.com/story/zelensky-deepfake-facebook-twitter-playbook/

Singh, Pallavi. 2015. *Aquaculture in India – Growing a New Industry*. https://www.swissre.com/dam/jcr:60f1c415-5369-4f85-a7a0-0678dcf719e6/Aquaculture_in_India_WEB.pdf

Singh, Saurabh, Pradip Kumar Sharma, Byungun Yoon, Mohammad Shojafar, Gi Hwan Cho, and In-Ho Ra. 2020. "Convergence of Blockchain and Artificial Intelligence in IoT Network for the Sustainable Smart City." *Sustainable Cities and Society* 63 (December): 102364. https://doi.org/10.1016/j.scs.2020.102364

Skiena, Steven S. 2017. *The Data Science Design Manual*. Springer.

Skokova, Yulia, Ulla Pape, and Irina Krasnopolskaya. 2018. "The Non-Profit Sector in Today's Russia: Between Confrontation and Co-optation." *Europe-Asia Studies* 70 (4): 531–563.

Smith, Dwight C. 1980. "Paragons, Pariahs, and Pirates: A Spectrum-Based Theory of Enterprise." *Crime & Delinquency* 26 (3): 358–386.

Snilstveit, Birte, Emma Gallagher, Daniel Phillips, Martina Vojtkova, John Eyers, Dafni Skaldiou, Jennifer Stevenson, Ami Bhavsar, and Philip Davies. 2017. "PROTOCOL: Interventions for Improving Learning Outcomes and Access to Education in Low-and Middle-Income Countries: A Systematic Review." *Campbell Systematic Reviews* 13 (1): 1–82.

Spiess-Knafl, Wolfgang. 2018. *You Had One Job – Transforming Social Security Systems into the Digital Work Age*. The European Liberal Forum (ELF) + NEOS LAB (editors).

Spiess-Knafl, Wolfgang, and Jessica Aschari-Lincoln. 2015. "Understanding Mechanisms in the Social Investment Market: What Are Venture Philanthropy Funds Financing and How?" *Journal of Sustainable Finance & Investment* 5 (3): 103–120.

Spiess-Knafl, Wolfgang, Clemens Mast, and Stephan Jansen. 2015. "On the Nature of Social Business Model Innovation." *Social Business* 5 (2): 113–130.

Spiess-Knafl, Wolfgang, and Barbara Scheck. 2019. *Social Enterprise Finance Market Analysis and Recommendations for Delivery Options*. Publications Office of the European Union.

Steinberg, Richard. 2006. "Economic Theories of Nonprofit Organizations." In *The Nonprofit Sector: A Research Handbook*, 117–139. Yale University Press.

Surden, Harry. 2019. "Artificial Intelligence and Law: An Overview." SSRN Scholarly Paper ID 3411869. Social Science Research Network. https://papers.ssrn.com/abstract=3411869

Sustainalytics. 2021a. "Second-Party Opinion: Public Power Corporation Sustainability-Linked Bond Framework (February 2021)." www.dei.gr/Documents2/BOND%202021/Public%20Power%20Corporation%20Sustainability-Linked%20Bond%20Framework%20Second-Party%20Opinion.pdf

———. 2021b. "Second-Party Opinion: Public Power Corporation Sustainability-Linked Bond Framework (June 2021)." www.dei.gr/Documents2/BOND%202021/BOND062021/Public%20Power%20Corporation%20Sustainability-Linked%20Bond%20Framework%20Second-Party%20Opinion%20Update%20.pdf

Swan, Melanie. 2015. *Blockchain: Blueprint for a New Economy*. O'Reilly Media, Inc.

Szabo, Nick. 1994. "Smart Contracts." https://www.fon.hum.uva.nl/rob/Courses/InformationInSpeech/CDROM/Literature/LOTwinterschool2006/szabo.best.vwh.net/smart.contracts.html

Tasca, Paolo, and Claudio J. Tessone. 2018. "Taxonomy of Blockchain Technologies." *Principles of Identification and Classification* 31. https://doi.org/10.5195/ledger.2019.140

TensorFlow. 2022. "Universal Sentence Encoder." www.tensorflow.org/hub/tutorials/semantic_similarity_with_tf_hub_universal_encoder

The Economist. 2021. "A Takeover in Britain Shows Shareholders Still Rule the Corporate Roost." *The Economist*, September 23, 2021. www.economist.com/business/2021/09/23/a-takeover-in-britain-shows-shareholders-still-rule-the-corporate-roost?utm_campaign=the-economist-today&utm_medium=newsletter&utm_source=salesforce-marketing-cloud&utm_term=2021-09-28&utm_content=article-link-6&etear=nl_today_6

Thomas, Lyn C. 2000. "A Survey of Credit and Behavioural Scoring: Forecasting Financial Risk of Lending to Consumers." *International Journal of Forecasting* 16 (2): 149–172.

Trentmann, Frank. 2016. *Empire of Things: How We Became a World of Consumers, from the Fifteenth Century to the Twenty-First.* Penguin UK.

Turing, Alan M. 1950. "Computing Machinery and Intelligence." *Mind* 59 (236): 433.

Udrea, A., G. D. Mitra, D. Costea, E. C. Noels, M. Wakkee, D. M. Siegel, T. M. de Carvalho, and T. E. C. Nijsten. 2020. "Accuracy of a Smartphone Application for Triage of Skin Lesions Based on Machine Learning Algorithms." *Journal of the European Academy of Dermatology and Venereology* 34 (3): 648–655. https://doi.org/10.1111/jdv.15935

United Nations Department of Economic and Social Affairs Disability. 2022. "Convention on the Rights of Persons with Disabilities (CRPD)." www.un.org/development/desa/disabilities/convention-on-the-rights-of-persons-with-disabilities.html

uPlanner. 2016. "How Machine Learning Techniques Improve Student Retention." https://uplanner.com/en/blog/machine-learning-y-retencion-estudiantil/

Van Laar, Ester, Alexander J. A. M. Van Deursen, Jan A. G. M. Van Dijk, and Jos De Haan. 2017. "The Relation between 21st-Century Skills and Digital Skills: A Systematic Literature Review." *Computers in Human Behavior* 72: 577–588.

Vardi, Nathan. 2020. "Netflix Shifts 2% Of Its Huge Cash Pile To Financial Institutions Serving Black Communities." www.forbes.com/sites/nathanvardi/2020/06/30/netflix-shifts-2-of-its-huge-cash-pile-to-financial-institutions-serving-black-communities/

Véliz, Carissa. 2020. *Privacy Is Power.* Random House Australia.

Venegas, Percy. 2021. "Blockchain Consortia for the Social Good: An Introduction for Non-Technical Audiences." In *Innovations in Social Finance: Transitioning Beyond Economic Value,* edited by Thomas Walker, Jane McGaughey, Sherif Goubran, and Nadra Wagdy, 319–346. Springer International Publishing. https://doi.org/10.1007/978-3-030-72535-8_15

Vickers, Ian, and Fergus Lyon. 2014. "Beyond Green Niches? Growth Strategies of Environmentally-Motivated Social Enterprises." *International Small Business Journal* 32 (4): 449–470. https://doi.org/10.1177/0266242612457700

Wallace-Wells, David. 2019. *The Uninhabitable Earth: Life after Warming.* Tim Duggan Books.

Webb, Justin W., Laszlo Tihanyi, R. Duane Ireland, and David G. Sirmon. 2009. "You Say Illegal, I Say Legitimate: Entrepreneurship in the Informal Economy." *Academy of Management Review* 34 (3): 492–510.

Weber, Olaf. 2014. "Social Banking: Concept, Definitions and Practice." *Global Social Policy* 14 (2): 265–267. https://doi.org/10.1177/1468018114539864

Weisbrod, Burton A., ed. 1998. *To Profit or Not to Profit: The Commercial Transformation of the Nonprofit Sector.* Cambridge University Press. https://doi.org/10.1017/CBO9780511625947

Williamson, Katie, Aven Satre-Meloy, Katie Velasco, and Kevin Green. 2018. "Climate Change Needs Behavior Change: Making the Case for Behavioral Solutions to Reduce Global Warming." *Arlington, VA: Rare.*

Wood, Gavin. 2014. "Ethereum: A Secure Decentralised Generalised Transaction Ledger." *Ethereum Project Yellow Paper* 151 (2014): 1–32.

World Bank. 2021. "World Bank Catastrophe Bond Provides Jamaica $185 Million in Storm Protection." Text/HTML. World Bank. www.worldbank.org/en/news/press-release/2021/07/19/world-bank-catastrophe-bond-provides-jamaica-185-million-in-storm-protection

World Food Programme. 2022. "Building Blocks." https://innovation.wfp.org/project/building-blocks

Yahaya, Adamu Sani, Nadeem Javaid, Fahad A. Alzahrani, Amjad Rehman, Ibrar Ullah, Affaf Shahid, and Muhammad Shafiq. 2020. "Blockchain Based Sustainable Local

Energy Trading Considering Home Energy Management and Demurrage Mechanism." *Sustainability* 12 (8): 3385. https://doi.org/10.3390/su12083385

Yu, Kun-Hsing, Andrew L. Beam, and Isaac S. Kohane. 2018. "Artificial Intelligence in Healthcare." *Nature Biomedical Engineering* 2 (10): 719–731. https://doi.org/10.1038/s41 551-018-0305-z

Zad, Samira, Maryam Heidari, Parisa Hajibabaee, and Masoud Malekzadeh. 2021. "A Survey of Deep Learning Methods on Semantic Similarity and Sentence Modeling." In *2021 IEEE 12th Annual Information Technology, Electronics and Mobile Communication Conference (IEMCON)*, 0466–72. IEEE.

Zahra, Shaker A., Eric Gedajlovic, Donald O. Neubaum, and Joel M. Shulman. 2009. "A Typology of Social Entrepreneurs: Motives, Search Processes and Ethical Challenges." *Journal of Business Venturing* 24 (5): 519–532.

Zetzsche, Dirk A., Douglas W. Arner, and Ross P. Buckley. 2020. "Decentralized Finance." *Journal of Financial Regulation* 6 (2): 172–203. https://doi.org/10.1093/jfr/fjaa010

Zolfaghari, Badri, and Geraldine (Dean) Hand. 2021. "Impact Investing and Philanthropic Foundations: Strategies Deployed When Aligning Fiduciary Duty and Social Mission." *Journal of Sustainable Finance & Investment* : 1–28. https://doi.org/10.1080/20430 795.2021.1907090

Zou, James, and Londa Schiebinger. 2018. "AI Can Be Sexist and Racist – It's Time to Make It Fair." *Nature* 559 (7714): 324–326. https://doi.org/10.1038/d41586-018-05707-8

Zuckerman, Gregory. 2019. *The Man Who Solved the Market: How Jim Simons Launched the Quant Revolution.* Portfolio.

INDEX

Printed in the United States
by Baker & Taylor Publisher Services

Printed in the United States
by Baker & Taylor Publisher Services